KATIE KOTEEN
& KATE KASBEE
of Well Vegan

FRUGAL VEGAN

*Affordable,
Easy & Delicious*
VEGAN COOKING

PAGE STREET
PUBLISHING CO.

PAGE STREET
PUBLISHING CO.

First published in 2017 by

Page Street Publishing Co.

27 Congress Street, Suite 105

Salem, MA 01970

www.pagestreetpublishing.com

Distributed by Macmillan, sales in Canada by The Canadian Manda Group.

20   19   18   17   3   4   5   6

ISBN-13: 978-1-62414-377-9

ISBN-10: 1-62414-377-6

Library of Congress Control Number: 2016961740

Book design by Page Street Publishing Co.

Photography by Allie Lehman

Cover design by Mette Hornung Rankin

Printed and bound in China

As a member of 1% for the Planet, Page Street Publishing protects our planet by donating to nonprofits like The Trustees, which focuses on local land conservation. Learn more at onepercentfortheplanet.org.

DEDICATION

To Amelia who eats everything and Taj who eats nothing. —Katie

For my closest friends and family and their growing enthusiasm
for green vegetables. —Kate

Contents

•◄•

Introduction

- • -

Convinced going vegan is the fastest way to burn through your grocery budget? Think again. We have some super savvy tips and tricks for saving money and eating healthy. And, lucky for you, we're willing to share. From batch cooking to freezing to buying in bulk to knowing where to shop and when, we'll show you just how easy it is to follow a plant-based diet without breaking the bank.

SMART SHOPPING

MAKE A SHOPPING LIST

You've heard it a million times, but it's absolutely the foundation of smart shopping—make a list, make a list, make a list! Writing out a shopping list before you leave for the grocery store or farmers' market will save you both time and money. When you have specific recipes in mind, you'll only buy what you need and will be able to avoid making impulse purchases. Stick to the list.

BUY FROM THE BULK BINS

Americans throw away an unbelievable amount of uneaten food simply because it spoiled before we were able to eat it. When you buy in bulk, you can purchase as much or as little as you need. Items you can buy in bulk include rice, grains, flours, pasta, soup mixes, beans, cereals, trail mixes, nut butters, sweeteners, dried fruits, nuts and seeds, spices, salts and peppercorns. Buying spices in bulk is our absolute favorite. They're guaranteed to be fresh and you can avoid investing too much money in something you'll use way too little of.

BUY GROCERIES ONLINE

When it comes to food, we're impulse shoppers. We go into the store for tofu and walk out with a giant salad, a bottle of organic wine and some fancy crackers we don't need. A great way to avoid this superfluous shopping is by using a service like Thrive Market—imagine an online version of Costco meets Whole Foods. All your pantry items at a discount, delivered right to your door for free. No more impulse purchases! And if that isn't enough, buying most of your pantry items online makes weekly shopping trips a breeze. Just a quick stop for fresh produce and a few odds and ends from the aisles.

VISIT ETHNIC MARKETS

When we want legit fresh tofu, we know just where to go. Our local Asian Market has the absolute freshest and best-priced tofu—it's all about supply and demand. If you haven't had (really) fresh tofu, it's a treat worth seeking out. Some of the freshest produce and spices are tucked away in your local ethnic markets for far less than you would pay at the bigger stores. Think chilis, curries, mushrooms and spices. It's a treasure trove of interesting and affordable items, just waiting to be discovered.

BIG BOX STORES

You might think that being vegan closes the door on big box discounts, like good old Costco. But think again! While you might not be able to hit up the snack bar—they've yet to offer a vegan option—you can totally make that membership count. In addition to loads of budget-friendly, organic produce, you can get great deals on pricey items like hemp seeds, cooking oils and nut butters.

WATCH THE SALES DAYS AND FLIERS

Almost every store has an online sales flier, and many include coupons. Before you make your list for the week, check ahead for what's on sale and take advantage! For example, every Friday our local market has a different item from a different department on sale at an exceptionally low price. Even if you don't make Friday your full-blown grocery-shopping day, you can still check the online sales flyer to see if you can score any goodies at a bargain. Just a few extra clicks before you head out can keep you on budget and eating well.

FOLLOW YOUR LOCAL STORES ON SOCIAL MEDIA AND SUBSCRIBE TO THEIR EMAIL LISTS

If you're like us, you need another email subscription about as much as you need a pet ferret. The only difference is that subscribing to your local supermarket's email newsletter could actually help you be your most frugal self. That was probably an Oprah-esque overstatement, but staying in the loop definitely has its advantages. If you spend more time on social media than email, opt to keep up with store specials via Facebook or Twitter. If there's a bargain to be had, you'll be there!

BUY PRODUCE IN PEAK SEASON

Buying in-season produce is not only delicious—it's also easy on your wallet. Fresh and ripe usually means there's a discount to keep that produce moving. Plan your meals with the season in mind and you'll find you're really making the most of peak freshness and excellent pricing. Fresh summer fruits freeze well for smoothies all year long.

TOFU PRESSING

If you're new to tofu pressing, get cozy for a little read. Nothing complex, but the first go around takes a bit of explanation. The idea behind the press is to get as much water as possible out of the tofu so it will soak up other flavors. You'll want to get a jumpstart on the pressing and soaking, because it can take a bit of time. But that time is almost entirely hands off, and you will be rewarded with extra tasty tofu.

So here's an overview of the tofu press stack: towel, tofu, towel, cutting board, heavy stuff.

Drain the tofu. Grab more than a few paper towels or a few clean dish towels. Place the towels on the counter: four layers of paper towel or fold the dish towel a few times to layer it up. Then place the tofu on the towels, followed by more towels and a cutting board. We like to use canned items to weight the board. Then just leave it to sit for about 30 to 60 minutes.

BATCH COOKING AND FREEZING

How much time do you spend in the kitchen every day? Between cooking dinner at night, making breakfast for yourself in the morning and packing a lunch to take to school or work, the answer is probably: way too much time. Most of us are on the go nonstop from the moment we wake up until our heads hit the pillow at night. Any time that can be salvaged should be used for fun stuff. Like catching up on your favorite TV show, enjoying a glass of wine and reading a book or playing outside. Not slicing and dicing vegetables and getting lost in a sea of dirty dishes.

Batch cooking is a not-so-secret phenomenon that makes maintaining a plant-based diet a breeze. You can eat healthy, delicious, inexpensive meals every day of the week while drastically reducing your time in the kitchen. Never again will a wilted bunch of broccoli (ahem, money) be tossed in the compost heap, because it's getting chopped and going right into the freezer. Just prep your meals for the week on one day; so instead of chopping onions Monday night, Tuesday night and again on Thursday night—you get it done in one shot! Spending a couple of hours (maximum) in the kitchen on one day a week beats the heck out of spending an hour in the kitchen every day of the week.

Once you get the flow of all the prep work, freezing is your next best friend in the time-saver department. One of the best things you can do to avoid eating out is kill the unplanned trips to the grocery store and plan your portion sizes. Yes, regulating portion sizes is a fantastic way to stay on budget and keep it slim. Plan your portion sizes and freeze the rest in perfectly portioned containers. All the conveniences of frozen meals like Lean Cuisine, but healthier and cheaper. Better yet, doubling a recipe takes just a fraction of the extra time it would take to make it twice. So when enchilada sauce is on sale, stock up and make a bunch! Make Friday night freezer night.

If this is all way too much to wrap your head around, not to worry. You can start small. Consider your schedule, and determine what day of the week you're most pressed for time. By planning ahead and cooking your meals just for that day, you're guaranteed a few extra hours to get all of your to-dos done while ensuring you sneak a few healthy meals in.

BATCH COOKING AND FREEZING PRO TIPS

- Take advantage of coupons and promotions at the grocery store. Is a local quality grocery store like Whole Foods having a massive sale on organic tomatoes? Buy as many as you can and make a huge batch of pasta sauce. Use half for dinner and freeze the rest.

- Label and date every bag and container before putting it in the freezer. After a few days or even weeks have passed, you may forget what that mysterious sauce is. Most things keep 3 to 6 months in the freezer.

- Cool items to room temperature before you freeze them, but don't leave anything out longer than two hours to prevent bacteria growth.

- For foods that need to be baked, use containers that can go from the freezer straight to the oven, like foil containers with lids.

- Use a food processor for chopping onions. A few quick pulses is much more efficient than cutting the tearjerkers by hand.

- Slightly undercook your vegetables before you freeze them. This will prevent them from getting mushy when you reheat them at mealtime.

- It costs less to run a full freezer. Pack it in and if you don't have enough to fill it up, freeze big bottles of water.

OTHER THINGS YOU CAN FREEZE

- Nuts and seeds: Buy in bulk and freeze what you won't use within a few weeks.

- Avocados: Slice them, pit or no pit (it doesn't seem to make a difference), and add a quick brush of lime juice to keep them nice and green.

- Bread: Sandwich bread, buns, breadcrumbs and baguettes. To serve frozen baguettes, wrap them in foil and bake in the oven for 15 to 20 minutes at 400°F (204°C), depending on the size of your baguette.

- Baked goods: Muffins, pancakes, waffles and cookies.

- Fruit: Great for fruit that's about to be too ripe. Freeze it for use in smoothies or muffins later.

- Soups: Make lunch-size portions to pull out of the freezer the night before.
- Vegetables: Chopped onions, carrots, celery and bell peppers; all perfect for making soups.
- Wine: Use ice cube trays and drop it in your next recipes.
- Homemade garden burgers

THESE RECIPES FREEZE WELL
- Pineapple Scones (page 114)
- Biscuits and Gravy (page 120)
- Zucchini Banana Bread Muffins (page 125)
- Creamiest Pinto Beans (page 136)
- Chunky Marinara Sauce (page 169)
- Spaghetti with Lentil "Meatballs" (page 43)
- Lentil Soup with Greens (page 90)
- Roasted Carrot Curried Soup (page 93)
- Chickpea Curry (page 96)
- Black Bean and Tempeh Chili (page 99)
- Minestrone (page 100)
- Easy Vegetable Broth (page 107)
- Roasted Cauliflower Soup with Lemon Parsley Pesto and Croutons (page 103)
- Mulligatawny Soup (page 106)
- Roasted Tomato and Garlic Soup (page 97)
- Easy Vegan Enchiladas (page 13)
- Walnut Brownie Cookies (page 180)
- Flaky Pie Crust (page 192)

FOR MORE SMART SHOPPING TIPS, SEE PAGE 192.

CHAPTER 1

The Whole Enchilada

Unless you were one of the fortunate few who grew up in a hippie commune, most of us spent our early years eating meals that revolved around meat as the main attraction. Rethinking the dinner entrée is something many vegans struggle with. These budget-friendly takes on some of your favorite classics (and a few new ones)—with fresh ingredients, lighter sauces and (ahem) no meat—bring modern vegan entrées into the spotlight.

If you need sure-fire crowd pleasers, give the Beer Battered Avocado and Black Bean Tacos with Chipotle Slaw (page 14) or the Easy Vegan Enchiladas (page 13) a try. Both are sure to satisfy the most discriminating omnivore. And, as an added bonus, the enchiladas freeze well—double the recipe and tuck one away for later.

Easy Vegan Enchiladas

Nut-free
Splurge: Top enchiladas with vegan cheese, fresh cilantro or sliced green onion
Serves 6 • 60 minutes to prepare

— • •

Enchiladas are probably the most indulgent of Mexican fare: warm, soft tortillas wrapped around a delicious gooey filling and baked until bubbly hot. While you'll be hard pressed to find vegan enchiladas at an authentic Mexican restaurant, you can replicate the same feel and flavors at home by using plant-based ingredients. The best part about this recipe is that it mostly requires pantry staples you can keep on hand for a last-minute dinner. Run to the store for an avocado, or some fresh cilantro and green onion, and you're set.

1 cup (120 g) TVP

1 cup (240 ml) boiling water

1 (15-oz [425-g]) can vegetarian refried beans

½ cup (72 g) frozen corn

½ cup (130 g) salsa

1 tbsp (8 g) taco seasoning

8 flour tortillas, taco size

½ cup (120 ml) green taco sauce

1 cup (240 ml) red enchilada sauce

1 ripe avocado

Vegan cheese, fresh cilantro or sliced green onion, for serving, optional

Preheat the oven to 350°F (177°C).

In a mixing bowl, combine the TVP and boiling water. Allow it to sit for 5 to 10 minutes. Meanwhile, in a separate bowl, mix the refried beans with the corn and salsa. Set aside. Once the water is fully absorbed, add the taco seasoning to the TVP. Mix well to combine. Add the seasoned TVP to the refried bean/salsa mixture and stir it all up.

Heat your tortillas in the microwave for 15 to 20 seconds, or until soft and pliable. Add 1 to 2 spoonfuls of green taco sauce to the middle of each tortilla, and then add a scoop of the refried bean/salsa/TVP mixture. Roll the tortillas up and place them seam-side down in a 9 x 13–inch (23 x 33–cm) glass baking dish. Pour the enchilada sauce on top to completely cover the enchiladas and bake for 20 minutes. Before serving, top the enchiladas with sliced avocado, vegan cheese, cilantro and green onion, if desired.

TIP: These enchiladas freeze well, so I often make a double batch. Cover the baking dish with plastic wrap and then foil. When you're ready to bake them, remove the plastic wrap and put the foil back on. Bake at 350°F (177°C) for about 40 to 50 minutes, or until the sauce starts to bubble. If you think of it ahead of time, you can always pull the enchiladas out of the freezer the night before and let them thaw in the refrigerator overnight. This will reduce your cook time to about 20 to 25 minutes.

Beer Battered Avocado and Black Bean Tacos with Chipotle Slaw

Nut-free, soy-free
Splurge: Fresh lime to finish the tacos
Serves 4 · 30 minutes to prepare

— • —

Reminiscent of the quintessential Baja fish taco, you'll swear you can feel the sand in your toes and the sun on your cheeks when you make these. It's almost necessary you have a cold Pacifico in hand, or at least a few on deck for once you're finished with the smoking hot oil.

1 cup (125 g) flour

½ tsp salt

½ tsp pepper

1¼ cups (300 ml) beer

1 lime

1 (15-oz [425-g]) can vegetarian refried black beans

1 tsp cumin

1 tsp oregano

1 cup (240 ml) canola oil

1 ripe avocado, cut into 12 equal slices

6 tortillas, taco size

Fresh lime, for serving, optional

CHIPOTLE SLAW

½ green cabbage head, sliced thin

3 carrots, shredded

¼ cup (60 ml) vegan ranch or mayo

¼ tsp chipotle

Start by making the beer batter. Combine the flour, salt, pepper, beer and lime in a medium bowl. Whisk until smooth. Set aside.

Next make the slaw. Combine the cabbage, carrots, ranch/mayo and chipotle. Set aside.

Start warming the black beans in a small pan over medium heat. Add the cumin and oregano.

Warm the canola oil in a small, heavy-bottomed saucepan over medium-low heat. If you have a thermometer, you'll want the oil around 350°F (177°C); otherwise, you can put the handle of a wooden spoon into the oil. When tiny little bubbles form around it, you know the oil is ready.

Dip the avocado slices in the batter, allowing excess to drip back into the bowl, and drop them (very carefully) into the hot oil. Cook in the oil for about a minute or until lightly golden brown. Transfer the avocado slices with a slotted spoon onto a paper towel–lined plate to soak up any excess oil. Continue the process in small batches until all the avocado slices have been cooked.

Warm the tortillas and start assembling: black beans, two slices of avocado and topped with the chipotle slaw.

Gooey Mushroom Quesadillas

Nut-free
Splurge: Serve quesadillas with guacamole
Serves 4 • 25 minutes to prepare

•‑•‑•

The quesadilla is one of those Mexican staples that's just impossible not to like. From the gooey filling to the perfectly crisp tortilla, all of the senses go into overdrive at first bite. Of course, the quesadilla itself is just part of the equation. If your budget permits, a healthy serving of pico de gallo and homemade guacamole sends this plant-based recipe off the charts. FYI: The "cheese" is best eaten when it's warm, so be sure to assemble and serve this dish right away.

8 oz (227 g) extra-firm tofu, drained

½ cup and 2 tbsp (150 ml) water

2 tbsp and 2 tsp (20 g) tapioca flour

1½ tbsp (14 g) nutritional yeast

1½ tsp (7 ml) lemon juice

¾ tsp garlic powder

¾ tsp salt

2 cups (151 g) baby portobello mushrooms, finely chopped

1 tsp red pepper flakes

4 whole wheat tortillas

Pico de gallo, for serving, optional

Guacamole, for serving, optional

To make the cheese, first press the tofu with several layers of paper towel to remove as much water as possible. Then, break the tofu into a few small pieces and add them to the bowl of a food processor, followed by the water, tapioca flour, nutritional yeast, lemon juice, garlic powder and salt. Blend until completely smooth.

Spray a medium skillet with cooking spray. Sauté the mushrooms until softened, about 3 minutes. Remove from heat and set aside. Transfer the cheese mixture to a small saucepan and stir constantly over low heat. The cheese will begin to clump and eventually become gooey. Add the red pepper flakes and continue stirring for another minute or so. Add the sautéed mushrooms to the cheese mixture and stir to evenly combine. Remove from heat.

Lay the tortillas flat and spread one half with a quarter of the cheese mixture. Fold the tortillas in half and press lightly to seal. Wipe the skillet you used to cook the mushrooms with a paper towel and re-coat with cooking spray. Return the skillet to medium heat and cook the quesadillas until lightly brown and crispy, about 2 minutes on each side. Repeat with the remaining three tortillas. Cut each quesadilla into four pieces and serve immediately with pico de gallo and guacamole, if desired.

BBQ Chickpea Sliders

Nut-free, soy-free
Splurge: Roasted sunflower seed topping
Serves 4–6 • 15 minutes to prepare

◄ ● ◄

Though they first debuted at White Castle, sliders have evolved to include pretty much anything served on a tiny bun. We took a plant-based approach with this recipe by using nothing but chickpeas, BBQ sauce and a few seasonings to create the savory, delicious filling on these bad boys. If it fits in your budget, don't skimp on the Pineapple Slaw (page 143). It adds just the right amount of sweetness and crunch for an irresistible party snack or summery dinnertime dish.

1 (15-oz [425-g]) can chickpeas, rinsed and drained

½ cup (120 ml) BBQ sauce

½ tsp garlic powder

¼ tsp chili powder

Salt, to taste

12 whole wheat slider buns

1 cup (340 g) Pineapple Slaw (page 143)

Roasted sunflower seeds, for serving, optional

Add the chickpeas, BBQ sauce, garlic powder and chili powder to a saucepan. Cook over medium heat for 10 to 15 minutes, stirring constantly and smashing about half of the chickpeas with the back of a fork or slotted spoon. Add water 1 tablespoon (15 ml) at a time if the mixture starts sticking to the bottom of the saucepan. Remove from heat and season with salt to taste.

To assemble, spread a spoonful of the BBQ chickpeas on the bottom portion of a whole wheat slider bun. Top with a scoop of Pineapple Slaw and sprinkle with roasted sunflower seeds for some extra crunch, if desired.

Sweet Potato Steaks with Chimichurri Sauce

Nut-free, soy-free, gluten-free
Splurge: none
Serves 2 • 20 minutes to prepare

＊ ● ＊

When the grill is calling your name, these sweet potato "steaks" will satisfy all of your cravings for something smoky. The only tricky part about this recipe is cutting the slabs into even slices. If you have a mandoline, this would be a great time to bring it out. Otherwise, you can use a sharp knife. A steady hand will ensure your sweet potatoes cook evenly and completely. Don't forget the Chimichurri Sauce (page 161)! The fresh herbs and acidic flavor complement the grilled sweet potato in a major way.

1 sweet potato, peeled

½ tbsp (7 ml) olive oil

¼ tsp sea salt

⅛ tsp black pepper

¼ tsp smoked paprika

½ cup (130 g) Chimichurri Sauce (page 161)

Heat your grill or a cast-iron pan to medium heat. Cut the sweet potato into ¼-inch (6-mm) slabs and place them in a bowl with the olive oil, salt, pepper and smoked paprika. Toss to evenly coat. Put the seasoned sweet potato "steaks" on the grill. Flip them once, grilling until tender, about 7 minutes. Serve immediately with our Chimichurri Sauce.

BLT with Sriracha Mayo

Nut-free
Splurge: Add sliced avocado to each sandwich for healthy fat and extra flavor
Serves 4 • 5 minutes to prepare

The BLT is a relatively simple, no-frills sandwich. Therefore, each of the components plays an important role in the overall taste and feel. There's no room for sub-par ingredients here! First you've got the bacon. Our tried and true method uses marinated rice paper, baked to crispy perfection. For the lettuce, romaine hearts work best due to their mild flavor and high crunch factor. As far as the tomato, we suggest the beefsteak variety for its ideal seed-to-flesh ratio. A smear of Sriracha Mayo (page 159) is optional, but highly recommended.

8 slices whole wheat bread

¼ cup (60 ml) Sriracha Mayo (page 159)

12 pieces Crispy Vegan Bacon (page 116)

4 hearts romaine leaves

2 beefsteak tomatoes, sliced

Sliced avocado, optional

Slather one side of all eight slices of bread with Sriracha Mayo. Divide the Crispy Vegan Bacon amongst four slices of the bread, followed by the lettuce and sliced tomato. Top with the avocado slices and remaining bread slices, then cut each sandwich into halves and serve.

Rainbow Sushi Rolls

Nut-free, gluten-free
Splurge: Add avocado and/or Orange Glazed Tofu (page 137) to sushi rolls, sliced into ¼-inch (6-mm) strips
Serves 2 • 20 minutes to prepare

━ • ━

At sushi restaurants, the selection of vegetable rolls is usually lacking in creativity and flavor. Not to mention, ordering enough to feel satisfied can be pretty damaging to your dinner budget. But we have good news! Now you can enjoy bite-sized Japanese food in the comfort of your kitchen with homemade sushi rolls. You don't need to buy any fancy equipment or supplies, either. With a kitchen towel, a bit of practice and a lot of patience, you'll be rolling sushi like a pro in no time.

4 nori sheets

3 cups (485 g) brown rice, cooked

1 cup (40 g) spinach, thinly sliced

½ carrot, thinly sliced lengthwise

½ cup (170 g) purple cabbage, shredded

4 green onion stalks, sliced lengthwise

5 cherry tomatoes, quartered and seeded

Avocado or Orange Glazed Tofu (page 137), optional

Soy sauce or tamari, for serving

Place one sheet of nori on a bamboo sushi mat or a clean kitchen towel. Top with about ½ cup (80 g) of rice. Spread evenly to cover the bottom two-thirds of the surface, leaving about one-third of the nori sheet uncovered at the top. You may want to keep a bowl of water nearby to wet your fingers—it helps to prevent the rice from sticking to your hands.

Add a few pieces of spinach, carrot, purple cabbage, green onion, tomato and, if you're using it, avocado or Orange Glazed Tofu in a horizontal strip across the bottom of the nori sheet, about 1 inch (25 mm) away from the edge.

To roll your sushi, lift the edge of the mat or kitchen towel closest to you up and over the fillings, tucking into the other side. Continue rolling, stopping to squeeze the roll lightly along its length often to keep it from getting loose.

Wet the top inch of the nori sheet with a bit of water to help it seal once you've rolled it all the way. Then, set the roll aside with the seam facing down while you prepare your other rolls. When they're all ready, cut the rolls into 1½-inch (38-mm) pieces with a very sharp knife. Serve immediately with soy sauce or tamari, if desired.

Roasted Potato and Zucchini Pizza

Nut-free, soy-free
Splurge: Add fresh basil to the arugula mixture
Serves 4–6 · 40 minutes to prepare

⁃ ● ◀

If you like to make your own pizza dough, have at it. I have a great little pizza place in my neighborhood that has the most amazing fresh dough for almost nothing. Most grocery stores also carry it for a few dollars or less. The prep for the recipe is minimal—the zucchini and potato rounds scream mandoline, but a knife works just as well for this savory delight of a pizza. Guaranteed you won't miss the cheese. —Katie

3–4 medium red potatoes, sliced in thin rounds

2½ tbsp (37 ml) olive oil, divided

Salt and pepper

1 medium zucchini, sliced in thin rounds

Pizza dough

1 cup (40 g) arugula

1 medium tomato, diced

Fresh basil, optional

1 tsp balsamic vinegar

TIP: This pizza is perfection cooked on an outdoor grill. If you haven't cooked pizza on a grill before, be sure to do a little research. There's definitely a technique.

Preheat the oven to 425°F (218°C). Line two baking sheets with parchment paper.

Toss the sliced potatoes in ½ tablespoon (7 ml) of olive oil and a little salt and pepper. Lay them out on a baking sheet. Repeat the process for the zucchini, and put them on the other baking sheet so you can give the potatoes a little extra time in the oven. You'll want to roast the potatoes about 15 minutes and the zucchini just barely 10 minutes.

Set the roasted vegetables aside to cool.

Preheat the oven to the highest heat.

Prepare the dough, rolling it out into your pizza shape. Drizzle with 1 tablespoon (15 ml) of olive oil and sprinkle with a little salt and pepper. Top with the roasted vegetables. I like to do an alternating potato-zucchini overlapping pattern starting at the outer edge of the dish and working concentrically towards the center.

Bake for about 8 to 10 minutes or until the crust is golden brown.

In a medium bowl, toss the arugula and tomato with the balsamic vinegar, adding ½ tablespoon (7 ml) olive oil with a little salt and pepper. Top the cooked pizza with the arugula salad and serve immediately.

Seared Polenta with Cherry Tomatoes

Nut-free, soy-free, gluten-free
Splurge: none
Serves 4 • 25 minutes to prepare

— • • —

If you've never tried polenta, this recipe is a terrific introduction. Polenta is basically mushy cornmeal that was historically served as peasant food in North America and Europe. Today, polenta is a staple of Northern Italian cuisine, and it happens to be super affordable. You'll find it packaged in a tube, probably in the pasta aisle at your grocery store. This recipe will certainly test your patience, as it's important not to move the polenta around as it cooks. Doing so will cause it to stick to the pan, and no one wants that.

2 tbsp (30 ml) canola oil, divided

1 lb (454 g) polenta, sliced into ½-inch (13-mm) rounds

1 pint (298 g) cherry or grape tomatoes

4 garlic cloves, thinly sliced

2 cups (80 g) fresh arugula or spinach

Preheat the oven to 175°F (80°C). Heat 1 tablespoon (15 ml) of canola oil in a non-stick pan over medium heat. Once the oil is shimmering and glides easily across the pan, carefully add the polenta slices. Cook the polenta until crispy and golden on each side, about 8 minutes per side. Resist the temptation to move the polenta around as it cooks! You may have to work in batches depending on the size of your pan.

When done cooking, transfer the polenta slices to a paper towel to drain excess oil. Then place the polenta slices on a baking sheet and put them in the oven to stay warm while you prepare the tomatoes.

Carefully wipe the pan clean and add another tablespoon (15 ml) of canola oil. Heat the pan over medium-high heat, and once hot, add the cherry tomatoes. The tomatoes will pop and sputter as they cook in the oil. This is what you want! Cook until the tomatoes blister and their skins are lightly charred, about 3 to 4 minutes. Gently press on the tomatoes with the back of a spatula to release their juices. Reduce the heat to medium-low and add the garlic. Cook for a minute or so, until the garlic is fragrant. Remove from heat and transfer the garlic and tomatoes to a bowl.

To assemble, divide the polenta between four plates and top with a scoop of cherry tomatoes and their juices, followed by a small handful of fresh arugula. Serve immediately.

Mediterranean Stuffed Peppers

Nut-free, soy-free
Splurge: Use 5 oz (142 g) fresh spinach instead of frozen
Serves 4–6 · 55 minutes to prepare

—•◀—

In my family, stuffed peppers have been on steady dinner rotation since the oldest kid could chew. Back then, of course, the filling consisted of little more than ground beef and rice. Oh, how far the stuffed pepper has come. This recipe is influenced by the flavors of the Mediterranean with couscous, garlic, tomatoes and fresh parsley. As far as the white beans, you can use whichever variety you can find—they're pretty interchangeable in this recipe. Don't forget to finish your peppers off with a drizzle of creamy Cucumber Tzatziki Sauce (page 164)! —Kate

3 red or yellow bell peppers

1 tsp and 1 tbsp (20 ml) olive oil, divided

½ red onion, diced (about 1 cup [151 g])

2 cloves garlic, minced

1 cup (185 g) cooked couscous

½ (10-oz [284-g]) package frozen spinach, thawed and drained

1 (15-oz [425-g]) can white beans, drained and rinsed

1 (15-oz [425-g]) can fire-roasted diced tomatoes

½ tsp dried oregano

½ tsp dried thyme

Salt and pepper

½ cup (20 g) fresh parsley, chopped

Cucumber Tzatziki Sauce (page 164)

Preheat the oven to 400°F (204°C). Slice the bell peppers in half vertically and remove the seeds. Lightly coat each pepper with 1 teaspoon olive oil and roast in a glass baking dish for 20 to 25 minutes. Remove the peppers from the oven and allow them to cool a bit while you prepare the filling.

Add 1 tablespoon (15 ml) of olive oil to a pan and heat over medium-low. When hot, add the onion and cook until it begins to soften, about 3 minutes. Then add the garlic and cook until fragrant, another minute or two. Stir in the couscous, spinach, white beans, fire-roasted diced tomatoes, oregano and thyme, and mix until incorporated. Season with salt and pepper to taste, and remove from heat.

Carefully spoon the filling into each half of the bell peppers. It's okay if some of the mixture spills onto the baking dish. Bake the peppers for 15 to 20 minutes, or until they're cooked through. Remove from the oven and sprinkle with fresh parsley just before serving. Top each pepper half with a drizzle of our Cucumber Tzatziki Sauce, if desired.

Cauliflower Steaks with Sautéed Greens

Nut-free, soy-free, gluten-free
Splurge: Serve with Simple Lentils (page 131) and/or Mushroom Gravy (page 166)
Serves 2 • 20 minutes to prepare

●•◖

This is a simple and ridiculously inexpensive recipe. We find that it's best served with Simple Lentils (page 131) and Mushroom Gravy (page 166) as a stack: a cauliflower steak covered with lentils and greens, and topped with mushroom gravy. You can also take any unused cauliflower florets and make a cauliflower mash by boiling the pieces until soft, draining and running them through the food processor with a little vegan butter, salt and pepper.

1 large head cauliflower

Sea salt and pepper

2 tbsp (30 ml) olive oil, divided

½ medium yellow onion, diced small

1 bunch kale or other hearty greens, stemmed and chopped

Simple Lentils (page 131) and Mushroom Gravy (page 166), for serving, optional

Remove the outer leaf and cut the bottom off the cauliflower so it sits flat on a cutting board. Cut two to three 1-inch (25-mm) cauliflower steaks from top to stem. Rinse them gently and pat dry. Sprinkle each side with salt and pepper.

Heat a cast-iron skillet over medium high heat with 1 tablespoon (15 ml) of olive oil. Once the skillet is hot, add the first cauliflower steak and cook without turning for 5 to 7 minutes. Flip the cauliflower, cover and cook another 5 to 7 minutes. Repeat with the other cauliflower steaks.

Set aside the cauliflower steaks, and add the last tablespoon (15 ml) of olive oil to the pan. Add the onion and sauté until just lightly browned, about 10 to 12 minutes. Add the kale and cook until barely wilted, 3 minutes. Season with salt and pepper to taste and top with Mushroom Gravy.

Tomatoes Filled with Rice

Nut-free, soy-free
Splurge: Substitute fresh basil in place of dried
Serves 4 • 90 minutes to prepare

▄ ● ▄

This is a classic Italian recipe, perfect as summer comes to a close and we have our first chilly days of fall. The traditional version uses risotto rice (Arborio), but any white short-grain rice will do.

4 large tomatoes

1 tbsp (15 ml) olive oil

1 small yellow onion, diced

⅓ cup (70 g) Arborio rice or any short-grain rice

¼ cup (60 ml) vegetable broth or water

1 tsp dried basil

½ tsp salt

Bread crumbs

Preheat the oven to 350°F (177°C). Line a 9 x 9–inch (23 x 23–cm) baking dish with parchment paper.

Cut just the tops off the tomatoes. A serrated knife works best. Then take a spoon and scoop all of the insides into a large bowl, so you have nice little tomato shells. Set aside.

In a large saucepan, warm the olive oil over medium heat. Add the onion and cook until soft, about 8 minutes. Add the rice and cook until the edges are translucent, about 4 minutes. Add all of the tomato insides, broth (or water), basil and salt. Simmer all of this for about 10 minutes.

Place the tomato shells into the prepared baking dish. Fill each tomato with the rice mixture. Top with bread crumbs. Bake for about an hour.

Remove the tomatoes from the oven and let them cool for at least 10 minutes before serving.

CHAPTER 2

Carb Party

Pasta is one of the foundations of a great frugal pantry. With a box of noodles and a few simple ingredients, you can quickly and easily whip up a healthy vegan dinner. From something as basic as spaghetti tossed in olive oil with some fresh herbs and vegetables, to fancier dishes like Lemon and Pea Risotto (page 47), it doesn't cost much to make a flavorful and satisfying meal.

Pasta is simple to prepare, but we do have a few tips for getting it right. Make sure you start with a large pot of (heavily) salted boiling water— think ocean salty. Once the water is vigorously boiling, drop in your pasta. If they're long strands, be sure to break them in half first for quick and even cooking. Some people think this is bad luck, but even the Italians do it! So we're not afraid. Make sure the water is back up to boiling again after you add the pasta by putting the lid on your pot and turning up the heat. Once the water returns to a boil, remove the lid and continue to boil until your pasta is al dente. Drain, and return your pasta to the pot for saucing and tossing.

Kale Pesto Pasta

Nut-free, soy-free
Splurge: Use walnuts instead of sunflower seeds
Serves 4 • 20 minutes to prepare

━ ● ◄

Creamy, rich pesto perfection with a pop of flavor from the fresh tomatoes. This easy recipe is sure to become a regular, ideal for a quick weeknight dinner.

½ bunch kale, de-stemmed and chopped

1 lb (454 g) pasta

½ cup (20 g) basil leaves, torn

½ cup (80 g) shelled, salted sunflower seeds

2 cloves garlic, chopped

½ lemon, juiced

¼ cup (38 g) nutritional yeast

¼ cup (60 ml) olive oil

Salt and pepper, to taste

1 pint (298 g) cherry tomatoes, halved

Bring a large pot of water to a boil. Add the kale and let it boil for just a minute or two. Use a slotted spoon to remove the kale from the water and place it in a colander to drain. Bring the water back up to a boil and add the pasta. Cook until al dente or according to package directions. Drain, reserving ½ cup (120 ml) of the cooking water. Return pasta to the pot.

Add the kale, basil, sunflower seeds, garlic, lemon and nutritional yeast to the bowl of a food processor or blender. Process until smooth, drizzling in the olive oil while the food processor runs. If your pesto is dry, add some of the cooking liquid 1 tablespoon (15 ml) at a time until desired consistency is reached. Season with salt and pepper to taste.

Pour the pesto over the pasta, stirring well to combine. Add the halved cherry tomatoes and stir to incorporate. Distribute amongst 4 bowls and serve warm.

TIP: To transition this recipe from summer to fall, toss the tomatoes in a little salt and olive oil and roast at 400°F (204°C) for about 30 minutes, or until the tomatoes are soft and just starting to caramelize.

Kale Stuffed Shells with Marinara ⭐

Nut-free, soy-free
Splurge: Sprinkle stuffed shells with ½ cup (90 g) vegan Parmesan before baking
Serves 4–6 · 50 minutes to prepare

◄ • ►

Everyone loves stuffed pasta shells smothered in marinara sauce. Though traditionally a vessel for cheese, our shells are stuffed with a creamy blend of white beans, sautéed kale and garlic for a healthier, lighter take on the traditional dish. Any white bean will work here, but we like cannellini beans for their ease of smashing. These shells also freeze quite nicely, making them ideal for a quick weeknight dinner.

12 oz (340 g) jumbo shells

1 tbsp and 2 tsp (25 ml) olive oil, divided

2 (15-oz [425-g]) cans white beans, drained and rinsed

2 cups (80 g) kale, de-stemmed and chopped

1 tbsp (15 ml) lemon juice

2 cloves garlic, minced

½ tsp salt

2½ cups (613 g) Chunky Marinara Sauce (page 169)

Vegan Parmesan cheese, optional

Cook the pasta according to package directions. Drain, rinse and drizzle the shells with 1 tablespoon (15 ml) of olive oil to prevent sticking. Set aside.

Preheat the oven to 400°F (204°C). Add the white beans to a large mixing bowl and smash them with the back of a fork or the bottom of a glass. Once you've reached a smooth consistency, set the bowl aside. On the stove, bring a pan to medium-low heat. Rinse the kale under cold water and, without drying it, add it to the pan. Cover and cook for 5 minutes, or until the kale is bright green and tender. Remove from heat and add the kale to the mashed white beans. Then stir in the lemon juice, garlic and salt. Mix to fully incorporate.

Pour 1 cup (245 g) of Chunky Marinara Sauce in the bottom of a 9 x 13–inch (23 x 33–cm) glass baking dish. Fill each of the jumbo shells with the bean mixture and place in the baking dish. You should be able to fill about 24 shells. Pour the remaining 1½ cups (368 g) of marinara sauce over the tops of the shells and sprinkle with vegan Parmesan, if desired. Bake in the oven for 20 minutes, or until the sauce is slightly bubbly. Serve warm.

Mushroom Stroganoff

Nut-free, soy-free
Splurge: none
Serves 4 · 40 minutes to prepare

— ● ● —

The very definition of comfort food, this Mushroom Stroganoff is ideal for chilly winter nights when all you want is a big bowl of carbs to warm the cockles of your heart. Traditionally a Russian meal with beef in the starring role, we updated this nineteenth-century classic and gave it a plant-based twist. With tender, sautéed portobello mushrooms and a dairy-free cream sauce, our version packs all the delicious flavor of the original dish without the sky-high calorie count.

2 tbsp (30 ml) olive oil

½ yellow onion, diced

2 garlic cloves, finely chopped

1 lb (454 g) baby portobello mushrooms, sliced

1½ cups (355 ml) vegetable broth

2 tsp (10 ml) soy sauce or tamari

1 tsp dried thyme

½ cup (60 g) Vegan Sour Cream (page 167)

2 tbsp (16 g) whole wheat flour

1 lb (454 g) farfalle pasta, cooked

Salt and black pepper, to taste

Fresh parsley, chopped

Heat the olive oil in a pan over medium heat. Add onion and garlic and cook until fragrant and the onion is soft, about 5 minutes. Then add the mushrooms and cook until they release their juices and become soft, about 7 minutes.

Stir in the vegetable broth, soy sauce or tamari and thyme, and stir to combine. Reduce heat to medium-low and simmer until the liquid has reduced by a third, about 10 minutes. Mix in the Vegan Sour Cream and flour. Continue to simmer until the sauce thickens, another 3 minutes. Remove from heat.

Cook the pasta according to package directions, until al dente. Drain, rinse and return the noodles to the pot. Pour the mushroom sauce over the pasta and stir to coat. Season with salt and black pepper to taste. Divide the pasta between 4 bowls and garnish with freshly chopped parsley. Serve immediately.

Spaghetti with Lentil "Meatballs"

Nut-free, soy-free
Splurge: none
Serves 3—4 • 90 minutes to prepare

— • —

Who remembers diving into a giant plate of spaghetti and meatballs as a kid? We all do! There's little more comforting than this Italian—American dish that defined so many Sunday night dinners. In our version, the "meatballs" get their heartiness from cooked lentils that are blended with the very spices your grandma probably used in her famous recipe. Baked just long enough to be crispy on the outside and moist on the inside, this dish will be a hit with vegans and omnivores alike.

1 lb (454 g) whole wheat spaghetti

½ cup (100 g) brown or green lentils

1½ cups plus 3 tbsp (400 ml) water, divided

1 tbsp (10 g) chia seeds

1 tbsp (15 ml) olive oil

½ cup (75 g) red onion, diced

2 garlic cloves, minced

¼ cup (28 g) shredded carrots

¼ cup (32 g) whole wheat flour

½ tsp dried basil

½ tsp dried oregano

¼ tsp dried fennel

¾ tsp salt

¼ tsp black pepper

Chunky Marinara Sauce (page 169), for serving

Cook the spaghetti according to package directions. Drain, rinse and set aside. Meanwhile, combine the lentils and 1½ cups (355 ml) of water in a medium saucepan. Bring to a boil, cover and reduce heat. Simmer for 15 to 20 minutes, or until the lentils are tender. Drain any excess water and add the lentils to the bowl of a food processor.

Combine the chia seeds and 3 tablespoons (45 ml) of water in a small bowl. Allow it to sit for about 5 minutes, or until the water is absorbed.

While you wait for your "chia egg" to form, heat the olive oil in a pan over medium heat. Add the red onion and cook until soft, about 5 minutes. Then add the garlic and carrots and sauté until soft, another 5 minutes. Add the onion mixture, whole wheat flour, basil, oregano, fennel, salt and pepper to the bowl of the food processor. Pulse a few times to combine the ingredients. Pour in the chia egg and pulse several more times to fully incorporate. Transfer the lentil mixture to a mixing bowl.

Preheat the oven to 425°F (218°C). Roll the lentil mixture into golfball-sized balls and place on a baking sheet lined with parchment paper. Lightly spray the meatballs with cooking spray and bake for 20 to 25 minutes, until they're dry to the touch. Allow the meatballs to cool slightly before serving. Then toss with the spaghetti and serve with our Chunky Marinara Sauce.

Spicy Broccoli and White Bean Pasta

Nut-free, soy-free
Splurge: Use broccolini instead of broccoli
Serves 4 • 20 minutes to prepare

➤ ◆ ◀

Weeknights, this pasta crushes it—a little spicy, a little creamy and so easy to bring together, wine glass in hand. Almost all of the ingredients are pantry staples, so all you have to think about ahead of time is broccoli (or broccolini if you want to make it fancy).

12 oz (340 g) pasta

2 cups (182 g) broccoli, cut in small florets

¼ cup (60 ml) olive oil

4 cloves garlic, minced

½ tsp red pepper flakes, plus more to taste

1 can white beans, rinsed and drained

Salt and pepper

Bring 2 quarts (1.9 L) of heavily salted water to a boil. Cook the pasta according to package directions. Add the broccoli to the boiling pasta water and cook for about a minute. Fish out the broccoli with a slotted spoon and set aside. Set aside 1 cup (240 ml) of pasta water before draining.

Heat the olive oil, garlic and red pepper flakes in a large saucepan over medium heat for about a minute. Add the lightly cooked broccoli and white beans. Cook for another 3 to 4 minutes.

Drain the pasta and add ½ cup (120 ml) of the reserved cooking water to the beans and broccoli, mashing some of the beans with a wooden spoon to make a creamier sauce. Continue to add the rest of the cooking water until the desired consistency is reached.

Add the pasta to the pan, stir to combine, and let it cook a few more minutes, adding more cooking water if needed. Add salt and pepper to taste.

Pasta with Roasted Tomatoes and Basil

Nut-free, soy-free
Splurge: Top with chopped, toasted walnuts before serving
Serves 4 • 40 minutes to prepare, mostly hands off

❥

What could be simpler and more delicious than a light summer pasta with fresh tomatoes? Our garden is always exploding with the sweetest tiny tomatoes and we can never have enough recipes to use them all up. If you want to add a little extra protein, canned white beans (drained and rinsed) are a superb complement. Just mix them in when you bring the cooked pasta and tomatoes together.

16 oz (454 g) cherry or grape tomatoes

¼ cup (60 ml) olive oil, divided

12 oz (340 g) pasta

3 cloves garlic, minced

Salt and pepper

1 bunch fresh basil

Toasted walnuts, for serving, optional

Preheat the oven to 425°F (218°C). Line a baking sheet with parchment paper.

Toss the tomatoes in 1 tablespoon (15 ml) of olive oil, then turn them out onto the baking sheet to cook for about 30 minutes or until the tomatoes are very soft.

Bring 2 quarts (1.9 L) of water and a generous amount of salt to a boil. Cook the pasta according to package directions, setting aside ¾ cup (177 ml) of pasta water before draining.

Return the pasta and ½ cup (120 ml) of pasta water to the pot over medium-high heat. Add the garlic, remaining olive oil, roasted tomatoes, salt and pepper to taste. Add more pasta water, if needed.

Add basil and serve.

Lemon and Pea Risotto

Nut-free, soy-free
Splurge: Substitute ½ cup (120 ml) dry white wine in place of the beer
Serves 4 · 40 minutes to prepare

◗ • ◖

A basic risotto recipe is so versatile and easy to assemble from pantry staples: It's a must-have for your repertoire. You can easily substitute the peas for just about anything in season and add any fresh herbs you have around. A light broth is best, as richer, darker vegetable broths will be overpowering and color your rice a dull dark yellow. Better yet, get crazy and make your own with our recipe for Easy Vegetable Broth (page 107) to ensure a bright, well-balanced risotto.

Other vegetable combinations: corn and roasted tomatoes, asparagus and lemon (spendy), zucchini and thyme, roasted butternut squash and sage, mushrooms and thyme

5 cups (1.2 L) light vegetable broth or no-chicken broth

3 tbsp (43 g) vegan butter, divided

1 small onion, finely diced

1½ cups (315 g) risotto rice (Arborio or Carnaroli)

½ cup (120 ml) beer

1 small lemon, juiced and zested

Salt and pepper

1 cup (200 g) frozen peas

Bring the vegetable broth to a simmer in a medium saucepan. Remove from the heat and cover.

In a large, heavy-bottomed pan (we like to use a Dutch oven), melt 2 tablespoons (29 g) of vegan butter. Add the onion and cook until soft, 8 to 10 minutes.

Add the rice and cook until the edges are translucent, stirring frequently with a wooden spoon, about 4 minutes. Add the beer and let the rice absorb it all.

Now add the warm vegetable broth and keep stirring gently, but you don't need to be all crazy about it. You can step away for a few minutes. Let the rice absorb the broth before adding the next cup (240 ml) and continue until the rice is tender but still firm. It should take between 15 and 20 minutes.

Add 1 tablespoon (15 ml) of the lemon juice, the last tablespoon (14 g) of vegan butter, salt and pepper. Stir vigorously with a wooden spoon until the rice really starts to get creamy, about a solid minute. Taste for lemon, salt and pepper, and adjust as needed. Stir in the frozen peas and let sit until peas are just thawed, 3 to 4 minutes.

Thai Peanut Noodles

Gluten-free
Splurge: Add fresh cilantro, bean sprouts and lime wedges for serving
Serves 4 · 45 minutes to prepare

▸ ◂ ▸

In Thailand, the only plant-based options available aside from veggies are noodles, noodles and more noodles. Oh, and maybe some rice. Luckily, I'm a noodle fanatic so I had no problem stuffing myself. Once I got home, I really missed my daily noodle fix and decided to create a version I can make whenever the craving strikes. Let me tell you, that craving strikes often. Depending on your budget, you can make a super-simple version of this recipe with nothing more than noodles and Thai Peanut Sauce, or a fancier version decorated with fried tofu, sautéed veggies and fresh herbs. —Kate

8 oz (227 g) extra-firm tofu, drained

2 tbsp (30 ml) canola oil

1 medium carrot, shredded

1 red bell pepper, thinly sliced

8 oz (227 g) stir-fry rice noodles

Thai Peanut Sauce (page 156)

¼ cup (13 g) green onion, sliced

Fresh cilantro, bean sprouts, lime wedge, for serving, optional

Press the tofu with several layers of paper towel to release as much water as possible. Cut the tofu into cubes or slice into 1-inch (25-mm) strips. Heat the canola oil in a pan over medium heat. Add the tofu and cook until golden and slightly crispy, about 5 minutes on each side. In the last 2 minutes of cooking, add the carrot and bell pepper. Cook until the veggies are just soft, and then remove the pan from the heat.

Cook the rice noodles according to package directions. While the noodles cook, prepare the Thai Peanut Sauce. Once the noodles are done, add them to the pan with the tofu, carrot and bell pepper. Turn to medium-low heat and slowly stir in the sauce. Cook until the sauce is completely mixed in and the noodles, tofu and veggies are heated through, 2 or 3 minutes. Add a splash of water to thin the sauce if necessary. Divide between 4 bowls and garnish with sliced green onion and other desired toppings.

Penne with Pumpkin
★ Cream Sauce

Nut-free, soy-free
Splurge: Garnish with crispy sage leaves
Serves 4 • 20 minutes to prepare

➤ ● ◀

By the time autumn rolls around each year, we're counting down the days until it's cool enough to cozy up in a big sweater. Around this time, the craving for pumpkin kicks in. You'll find it in lattes, muffins and soups—salsas, sandwiches and even beer. Us? We like to put it in our pasta. This pumpkin cream sauce is warm, savory and perfectly suited to sweater season. For those who aren't fond of coconut, fear not. The taste is barely detectable beneath the flavorful layers of pumpkin, garlic and paprika.

1 lb (454 g) penne pasta

1½ tbsp (22 g) vegan butter

2 garlic cloves, minced

1 (15-oz [425-g]) can pumpkin purée

1 (13½-oz [382-g]) can coconut milk

¾ tsp paprika

¾ tsp salt

*Fresh or crispy sage leaves,
for serving, optional*

Cook the pasta according to package directions. Meanwhile, melt the vegan butter in a large saucepan over medium heat. Add the garlic and sauté for a minute or two, until fragrant. Stir in the pumpkin purée, coconut milk, paprika and salt.

Reduce heat to medium-low and simmer for 5 to 10 minutes, or until the sauce has thickened. Drain and rinse your pasta and combine it with the pumpkin cream sauce. Stir to thoroughly combine, garnish with fresh or crispy sage leaves if using, and serve immediately.

CHAPTER 3

Bring on the Bowls

Bowls are one of the most versatile vegan dishes you can add to your repertoire. Many of the ingredients are easily swapped out for whatever you might have on hand, growing in your garden or for seasonal on-sale items. Bowls are a great option for weeknight dinners and make for easy leftovers throughout the week.

The formula for most bowls goes a little something like this: grain, protein, vegetables, healthy extras, sauce and done! You can make your bowl as plain or dressed up as you'd like. There are so many possibilities! The recipes that follow are just a few of our favorites.

Burrito Bowl with Cilantro Tahini

Nut-free, soy-free, gluten-free
Splurge: Serve with fresh salsa, hemp seeds
Serves 4 • 45 minutes to prepare

◂ ● ◂

Is there anything more beautiful than a burrito bowl? You get to enjoy all of the stuff that makes a burrito delicious—rice, veggies, beans, avocado and salsa—without making a complete mess as you eat it. We boosted the healthy factor of this Mexican-inspired meal by adding kale and carrots, followed by a drizzle of zesty Cilantro Tahini (page 152)—a terrific source of B vitamins. And, if you feel like splurging, hemp seeds will provide you with your daily dose of omega-3 fatty acids.

1 cup (210 g) short-grain brown rice

2 medium carrots, cut into ½-inch (13-mm)–thick rounds

1 bunch kale, de-stemmed and chopped

1 (15-oz [425-g]) can black beans, rinsed and drained

½ cup (72 g) frozen corn, defrosted

1 avocado, diced

¼ cup (60 ml) Cilantro Tahini (page 152)

Cook the rice according to package directions. Once the water has been completely absorbed, remove the rice from heat and fluff with a fork. Meanwhile, fill another pot with a couple of inches of water and bring to a boil. Put the carrots in a steamer basket and place it over the boiling water. Cover the pot and cook the carrots for 3 to 5 minutes. Then, add the kale to the steamer basket and cook until barely soft and bright green, another 4 to 5 minutes. Remove the carrots and kale from heat and set aside.

Warm the black beans in a small saucepan on the stove or in the microwave. Defrost the corn in the microwave and dice your avocado. Add a scoop of brown rice to each bowl, followed by the black beans, carrots, corn, kale, avocado and a drizzle of Cilantro Tahini. Serve immediately.

Tofu, Sweet Potato and Spinach Bowl with Miso Garlic Dressing

Nut-free
Splurge: Top with chopped, toasted walnuts before serving
Serves 4 • 40 minutes to prepare

◄ ● ►

This is one of our absolute favorite things to make when those cold winds start blowing. The smell of the roasted sweet potatoes wafting through the house, barley simmering on the stove—fall perfection. If you want to add some extra flavor to your tofu, press and soak it in vegetable broth. You can check out instructions for pressing and soaking tofu on page 7.

1 cup (185 g) pearled barley

2 sweet potatoes, peeled and cut into 1-inch (25-mm) pieces

2 tbsp (30 ml) olive oil, divided

1 (15-oz [425-g]) container extra-firm tofu, patted dry and cut into 1-inch (25-mm) pieces

8 oz (227 g) fresh spinach

Salt and pepper

Miso Garlic Dressing (page 155)

Toasted walnuts, for serving, optional

Preheat the oven to 400°F (204°C).

Start cooking the pearled barley according to package directions.

Line two baking sheets with parchment paper, one for the sweet potatoes and one for the tofu. Roast for 20 minutes, flip the pieces over and cook for another 10 minutes. Take out the sweet potatoes when they're soft and slightly browned on the bottom. At this time, you'll want to add the tofu to the oven as well. Using the same bowl as the sweet potatoes, toss the tofu cubes gently in 1 tablespoon (15 ml) of olive oil and turn out onto the second baking sheet. Check tofu after 10 minutes and flip the pieces if needed. Take out the tofu when it starts to brown on the bottom.

Layer the cooked barley, fresh spinach, sweet potatoes and tofu in a bowl. Top with salt and pepper, dressing and toasted walnuts.

Falafel Bowl
with Israeli Couscous

Nut-free, soy-free
Splurge: none
Serves 4 · 50 minutes to prepare

► ● ◄

Falafel is fun to say and even more fun to eat. Making it from scratch is pretty enjoyable, too! This recipe is a good one to make with kids, as there isn't much to it aside from throwing your ingredients into a food processor and rolling the mixture into balls. Of course, you'll want to leave the frying to an adult who can reach the stove. Crispy on the outside and moist on the inside, these falafel are a great supplement to salads and wraps in addition to the bowl below. Don't hesitate to double the recipe and freeze half for later!

2 cups (402 g) dried chickpeas, soaked
8–12 hours

⅛ cup (5 g) chopped fresh parsley

4 cloves garlic, minced

½ yellow onion, chopped

1½ tsp (4 g) cumin

1 tsp ground coriander

1 tbsp (8 g) whole wheat flour

½ lemon, juiced

¼ tsp cayenne pepper

1½ tsp (8 g) sea salt, plus more to taste

¼ tsp black pepper

2 tbsp (30 ml) canola oil, for frying

2 cups (370 g) couscous, cooked

4 cups (188 g) baby spinach

1 cup (119 g) cucumber, thinly sliced

1 cup (149 g) cherry tomatoes, halved

½ cup (58 g) radishes, thinly sliced

1 cup (240 ml) Cucumber Tzatziki
Sauce (page 164)

Combine the chickpeas, parsley, garlic, onion, cumin, coriander, flour, lemon juice, cayenne pepper, salt and pepper in a food processor. Blend until the chickpeas have been reduced to a fine paste and the ingredients are fully combined. Resist the temptation to add water! If the mixture feels dry, continue to process. The consistency should be just moist enough that you can squeeze a bit of the mixture between your fingers and it holds its shape. Transfer the falafel mixture to a mixing bowl and set aside.

Heat 2 tablespoons (30 ml) of canola oil in a pan over medium heat, and line a plate with a few paper towels. Roll the falafel mixture into golfball-size balls and carefully place them in the pan, using the back of a spatula or fork to slightly flatten each patty. Cook the falafels for 3 to 5 minutes on each side, or until crispy and golden brown, working in batches and adding more oil as needed. When done, transfer each falafel to the paper towel–lined plate to drain any excess oil.

Divide the couscous, baby spinach, cucumber, cherry tomatoes and radishes between 4 bowls. Top with a few falafel pieces and a drizzle of Cucumber Tzatziki Sauce. Serve immediately.

Backyard BBQ Bowl

Nut-free, gluten-free
Splurge: Use quinoa instead of brown rice
Serves 4 • 1 hour and 40 minutes

There's no need to wait until Memorial Day to enjoy the smoky, savory flavors of a barbecue. This recipe invokes all the flavors of summer and ties them into one tidy bowl you can enjoy any time of year. For the chickpeas, you can make your own Cajun seasoning from spices you already have at home, or buy a pre-made blend to keep things simple. Whatever you do, make sure you reserve some extra BBQ sauce for drizzling.

1 cup (211 g) brown rice, uncooked

1 (15-oz [425-g]) package extra-firm tofu, drained

½ cup (120 ml) BBQ sauce

1 (15½-oz [439-g]) can chickpeas, drained and rinsed

½ tbsp (7 ml) olive oil

1 tsp Cajun seasoning

2 cups (290 g) corn kernels

4 cups (268 g) kale leaves, torn

1 cup (149 g) cherry tomatoes, halved

1 avocado, diced

Sliced green onion and fresh cilantro, for serving, optional

Cook the rice according to package directions and set aside. Meanwhile, prepare the tofu. Press the tofu with a few layers of paper towel to remove as much water as possible. Then cut the tofu into 1-inch (25-mm) cubes. Place the tofu cubes in a shallow baking dish and drizzle with the BBQ sauce. Toss gently to evenly coat, and allow the tofu to marinate for 1 hour.

Preheat the oven to 400°F (204°C). Using a slotted spoon, transfer the tofu to a baking sheet lined with parchment paper and bake for 20 minutes. Flip the tofu and put it back in the oven for another 10 to 15 minutes. Meanwhile, toss the chickpeas with olive oil and Cajun seasoning. Warm for 1 minute in the microwave or in a small saucepan over low heat. Defrost corn kernels in a microwave-safe bowl. Rinse the kale with water and squeeze dry. Add to a dry skillet over medium heat and cook until the water droplets evaporate and the kale is slightly wilted, about 2 minutes.

To assemble, add a scoop of brown rice to the bottom of each bowl. Layer with BBQ tofu, chickpeas, corn, kale and cherry tomatoes. Top it off with diced avocado and garnish with extra BBQ sauce, green onion and cilantro leaves, if desired.

Warm Fall Harvest Bowl

Nut-free, soy-free
Splurge: Garnish with toasted pumpkin seeds
Serves 4 · 40 minutes to prepare

— • —

This bowl tastes and feels like a warm hug. It has all the makings of a perfect fall meal, right down to the root vegetables drizzled in maple syrup and cinnamon, roasted to tender perfection. The farro offers a nice change in texture from brown rice or couscous, but you can really use any grain you have in your pantry. Top it all off with fresh, diced apple and toasted pumpkin seeds for an autumnal meal you'll return to again and again.

1 cup (185 g) farro, uncooked

2 tbsp (30 ml) balsamic vinegar

1 tbsp (15 ml) coconut oil

2 tbsp (30 ml) maple syrup

1 tsp cinnamon

⅛ tsp cayenne pepper

¼ tsp salt

2 cups (280 g) butternut squash, cut into 1-inch (25-mm) cubes

2 cups (256 g) carrot, cut into 1-inch (25-mm) cubes

1 cup (152 g) onion, cut into 1-inch (25-mm) chunks

6 cups (402 g) kale, torn

1 cup (180 g) apple, diced

Toasted pumpkin seeds, for serving, optional

Cook the farro according to package directions. Drain any excess water and transfer the farro to a large mixing bowl. Add balsamic vinegar and mix to combine. Set aside to cool.

Preheat the oven to 450°F (232°C). Combine the coconut oil, maple syrup, cinnamon, cayenne pepper and salt in a small bowl. Whisk to combine. Transfer the squash, carrot and onion to a baking sheet and arrange in a single layer. Drizzle the coconut oil mixture over the veggies and toss to completely coat each piece. Bake for 20 minutes, giving the veggies a good stir and a flip halfway through. When the veggies are fork tender, remove them from the oven and set aside.

Heat a pan over medium-low heat. Rinse the kale in a colander and drain, but do not dry. Add the kale to the hot pan and cook for a minute or two, until the kale has wilted and the water has evaporated. Remove from heat. Divide the farro between 4 bowls. Top with kale and roasted veggies. Stir in diced apple and top with toasted pumpkin seeds, if desired. Serve warm.

Cuban Black Bean Bowl

Nut-free, soy-free, gluten-free
Splurge: Top with fresh cilantro
Serves 4–6 • 2 hours to prepare, mostly hands off

— • ◄

If you're a plantain newcomer, a perfectly ripe plantain has a peel that's nearly black on the outside. You'll want one that still has some yellow splotches, so it's a little more firm. If you're short on time, keep in mind that 3½ cans of beans is about equal to 1 pound (454 g) dried beans.

1 lb (454 g) dried black beans

1 large green bell pepper, stemmed and seeded, diced small and divided

8 garlic cloves, minced and divided

1 bay leaf

Sea salt and pepper

2 tbsp (30 ml) olive oil

1 onion, diced

1½ tsp (1 g) dried oregano

1 tsp cumin

1½ tsp (4 g) smoked paprika, optional

1½ tbsp (22 ml) apple cider vinegar

¼ cup (60 ml) vegetable oil

2 medium plantains, cut in ¼-inch (6-mm) rounds

Cilantro Lime Rice (page 146)

Put the dried beans in a large bowl and cover with 2 to 3 inches (50 to 75 mm) of water. Soak for at least 6 hours.

In a large pot, combine the beans, half the bell pepper, 4 of the garlic cloves, bay leaf and 2 teaspoons (10 g) of salt. Cover with 8 cups (1.9 L) of water and bring to a boil. Cover the pot and simmer until the beans are tender, 60 to 90 minutes.

Heat the olive oil in a skillet over medium-high heat. Add the rest of the bell pepper and onion. Cook until softened, about 10 minutes. Add the last 4 cloves of garlic, oregano, cumin, smoked paprika and 1 teaspoon salt, and stir for another minute. Pour in the vinegar, scraping the bottom of the pan with a wooden spoon. Add to the beans.

Bring the beans to a boil over medium heat. Then lower to a simmer and cook, uncovered, for 20 minutes or so, skimming any foam from the top. Add salt and pepper to taste.

While the beans are cooking, heat a few tablespoons of vegetable oil in a large skillet over medium heat. Add a single layer of plantains to the oil, pressing them down with a metal spatula. Turn the slices as they brown, about 2 to 3 minutes per side. Drain on a paper towel–lined plate, and salt lightly.

Serve the beans with Cilantro Lime Rice and plantains.

TIP: Easily skim the foam off of the beans by gently swirling a ladle in the middle of your cooking pot. All of the foam will gravitate to the edges and can easily be scooped away with a spoon.

Ratatouille Bowl with Creamy Polenta

Nut-free, soy-free, gluten-free
Splurge: Serve topped with fresh basil
Serves 4 · 60 minutes to prepare

◄ ● ◄

All of the essentials of a traditional ratatouille, without all the fuss. This simplified version doubles as an incredibly rich and hearty pasta sauce when you don't have time to make polenta. The best part of this recipe is that the chopping can be quite rough and it still looks charmingly rustic.

1 small eggplant, diced in 1-inch (25-mm) cubes

1 red bell pepper, cut in 1-inch (25-mm) pieces

1 zucchini, diced in 1-inch (25-mm) cubes

1 yellow squash, diced in 1-inch (25-mm) cubes

½ red onion, cut in 1-inch (25-mm) pieces

1 tbsp (15 ml) olive oil

1 tsp basil

1 tsp thyme

1 tsp rosemary

1 tsp oregano

1 tsp salt

1 (15-oz [425-g]) can diced or crushed tomatoes

1 cup (210 g) dried polenta

Fresh basil, for serving, optional

Preheat the oven to 425°F (218°C).

Combine the eggplant, red bell pepper, zucchini, yellow squash and red onion in a large bowl. Toss with the olive oil. Combine the spices and toss with the vegetables.

Pour ¼ cup (40 g) of the diced tomatoes in the bottom of a 9 x 12-inch (23 x 30–cm) baking dish. Turn the dish to evenly coat the bottom. Add the vegetables and top with the remaining tomatoes. Bake for 30 to 40 minutes or until the vegetables are soft and starting to brown.

Meanwhile, in a medium saucepan (preferably with a heavy bottom) bring 5 cups (1.2 L) of water and 1 teaspoon of salt to a boil over medium heat. Reduce heat to low, add the polenta and whisk constantly for about 3 minutes, or until the polenta thickens.

Continue to cook the polenta over low heat for another 45 to 50 minutes. You'll need to stir it every 10 minutes or so to keep it from burning or sticking to the bottom. If the polenta becomes too thick, which it will unless you're some sort of polenta wizard, add ½ cup (120 ml) of water to loosen it up and continue cooking until the polenta is soft. There's no al dente with polenta; it should be creamy and not taste raw. Spoon the polenta into 4 bowls, top with a generous amount of ratatouille and serve.

TIP: If you want a richer flavor in your polenta, use vegetable broth in place of half of the water.

Crispy Buffalo Tofu Bowl

Nut-free
Splurge: Top with fresh chives
Serves 4 • 45 minutes to prepare, plus time for pressing tofu

◄ • ◄

There are few culinary combinations more American than fried "chicken" and mashed potatoes: the ultimate comfort food pairing. You'll want to set aside some time for the tofu prep, but not to worry—it's almost entirely hands off. The rest of the recipe comes together quickly. With a little planning and a touch of multi-tasking, you'll be digging in to some down-home goodness in no time.

5–6 medium-sized potatoes, peeled and diced

2 tbsp (29 g) vegan butter

¼ cup (60 ml) nondairy milk or creamer

Salt and pepper

16 oz (454 g) firm or extra-firm tofu, drained and pressed (see page 7)

2 cups (473 ml) vegetable broth

¼ cup (55 g) vegan mayo

2 tbsp (30 ml) hot sauce (I like Cholula brand)

¼ cup (38 g) cornstarch

1 cup (120 g) panko bread crumbs

¼ cup (60 ml) canola oil

1 cup (145 g) frozen corn

Mushroom Gravy (page 166)

Fresh chives, for serving, optional

Place the potatoes in a large pot, cover with water and bring to a boil. Cook, uncovered, for 10 to 15 minutes or until the potatoes are tender. Drain and return to the pot. Add the vegan butter and nondairy milk. Mash with a potato masher and season with salt and pepper.

After your tofu is drained and pressed, cut the block in half and immerse it in the vegetable broth. We use a container, such as Tupperware, that's just slightly larger than our tofu block. Let that sit for an hour or two in the fridge.

Remove the tofu from the vegetable broth and drain to remove any excess liquid. Cut the tofu into about 16 equal strips.

In a small bowl, mix the mayo and hot sauce. You'll also want to have the cornstarch and panko in separate bowls for your dipping assembly line.

Dip the tofu strips in cornstarch, buffalo mayo and finally panko bread crumbs, in that order.

Heat half of the oil in a medium nonstick or cast-iron pan. Add the tofu strips, turning to brown on all sides, 3 to 4 minutes per side. Set on a paper towel–lined plate to drain off any excess oil. You may need to do a few batches and add additional oil to work through all of your strips.

Warm your frozen corn on the stovetop or in the microwave and make the gravy. Finally, assemble your bowl: mashed potatoes, crispy buffalo tofu, corn and gravy.

CHAPTER 4

Best Dressed Salads

Salads are often overlooked because they're assumed to be boring, bland and unsatisfying. While we've certainly eaten our fair share of disappointing salads, we've also had some really great ones. From tender grains to hearty legumes and grilled veggies to zesty vinaigrettes, adding complex flavor and texture to leafy greens can give new life to an otherwise underwhelming dish.

Coming up next, you'll find exciting salad recipes that will change everything you thought you knew about eating your veggies. A few of our personal favorites include the Grilled Romaine and Beet Salad (page 74) and the Crunchy Thai Salad (page 77). Each of these dishes is hearty enough to stand alone as an entrée. If you want to reduce the portion size to feed a few more mouths, we suggest serving your greens with a side of warm and filling soup, stew or chili.

Bruschetta Pasta Salad

Nut-free, soy-free
Splurge: Mix in ⅓ cup (60 g) vegan Parmesan cheese before serving
Serves 10—12 • 2 hours to prepare

● ● ◖

In the heat of summer, your garden is overflowing with tomatoes and basil. Don't let your backyard bounty go to waste! We deconstructed traditional bruschetta and turned it into a pasta salad that will please even the pickiest eaters at your potluck. The key to making this dish super-flavorful is marinating those tomatoes. Because they're infused with olive oil, garlic and balsamic vinegar, there's no need to add dressing before serving.

1 lb (454 g) medium shell pasta

1 tbsp and 1 tsp (20 ml) olive oil, divided

3 garlic cloves, minced

1 tbsp (15 ml) balsamic vinegar

½ tsp salt

½ tsp black pepper

2 pints (596 g) cherry or grape tomatoes, halved

2 cups (80 g) baby spinach, thinly sliced

½ cup (20 g) fresh basil, thinly sliced

Vegan Parmesan cheese, for serving, optional

Cook the pasta according to package directions, until al dente. Drain and rinse with cold water. Drizzle the pasta with 1 tablespoon (15 ml) of olive oil, mix to thoroughly coat and set in the fridge to chill. Meanwhile, combine the remaining teaspoon of olive oil with the garlic, balsamic vinegar, salt and pepper in a large mixing bowl. Add the tomatoes and toss to coat. Set in the fridge and allow the tomatoes to marinate for 1 to 2 hours.

Just before serving, add the pasta to the tomatoes. Stir in the spinach and basil. Toss to combine and adjust seasonings to taste. Serve cold.

Grilled Romaine and Beet Salad

Soy-free, gluten-free
Splurge: none
Serves 4 • 30 minutes to prepare

● ● ●

Whoever decided salad has to be served cold has clearly never tried putting their lettuce on the grill. I picked up this technique in my culinary program and have since used it to impress many friends and family members. If you toss the beets on the grill first, they'll be tender just in time to serve atop your lightly charred romaine. Finish it off with a simple citrus dressing and you've got a refreshing salad perfectly suited for barbecue season. —Kate

2 cups (272 g) beets, peeled and sliced into rounds

3 tsp (15 ml) olive oil, divided

¼ tsp sea salt

⅛ tsp black pepper

2 romaine hearts

¼ cup (23 g) sliced almonds

¼ cup (60 ml) Orange Chia Dressing (page 162)

Preheat your grill to medium heat. Coat the beet slices with 1 teaspoon of olive oil and season with a pinch of salt and pepper. Put the beets on a large piece of aluminum foil and seal into a packet. Put the foil packet on the grill and cook 20 to 25 minutes, or until the beets are tender.

Meanwhile, slice the romaine hearts in half lengthwise and brush the cut sides with olive oil. Season with sea salt and black pepper. Set the romaine hearts on the grill cut side down and cook until slightly charred. Flip the romaine hearts over and grill for a minute or two on the other side.

Remove from heat and set aside to cool. Serve the romaine cut side up with beets, almonds and a drizzle of Orange Chia Dressing.

Curried Potato Salad

Soy-free
Splurge: none
Serves 6 · 1 hour to prepare

— • —

This recipe was inspired by a trip to a local grocer's salad bar, although their version used fried tofu instead of potatoes. This recipe is much less polarizing—no one will guess it's vegan! Perfect as a side dish for a summer potluck or barbecue, our Curried Potato Salad can be thrown together quickly and scaled up to feed a crowd. While we highly recommend the diced apple for the crunch-factor, you can substitute golden raisins to achieve the same level of sweetness.

1½ lb (680 g) red potatoes, scrubbed

1 medium carrot, shredded

3 green onions, chopped

1 medium apple, diced

½ cup (120 ml) Curry Dressing (page 163)

¼ cup (23 g) sliced almonds

Sea salt and pepper, to taste

Cut the potatoes into bite-size chunks. Put the potatoes in a pot and cover them with an inch (25 mm) of water. Bring the water to a boil and cook the potatoes for about 5 minutes, or until fork tender. Drain the potatoes and rinse with cold water. Once they're not steaming anymore, place them in the refrigerator to cool.

Meanwhile, prepare your carrot, green onions and apple. Mix them together in a large serving bowl and stir in the potatoes once they've cooled. Drizzle your potato salad with the Curry Dressing and top with sliced almonds. Mix thoroughly and add sea salt and pepper to taste. Chill in the refrigerator until ready to serve.

Crunchy Thai Salad

Soy-free, gluten-free
Splurge: Swap quinoa for millet or add 1 cup (155 g) edamame for extra protein
Serves 4 • 30 minutes to prepare

▪ ● ◂

You might recognize millet as the main ingredient in birdseed, but we find it much more enjoyable when mixed with crisp veggies and smothered in peanut sauce. While quinoa is often celebrated as the best gluten-free grain for filling out salads, millet is equally delicious and much more affordable. In fact, the swap is pretty seamless in terms of taste and texture!

¾ cup (140 g) uncooked millet

2 cups (681 g) purple cabbage, shredded

1 cup (110 g) carrots, shredded

1 cup (100 g) sugar snap peas, thinly sliced

½ cup (20 g) cilantro, chopped

¼ cup (13 g) green onion, thinly sliced

Edamame, optional

½ cup (120 ml) Thai Peanut Sauce (page 156)

½ cup (75 g) roasted and salted peanuts, crushed

Cook the millet according to package directions. Fluff with a fork and set aside to cool. Add the purple cabbage, carrots, sugar snap peas, cilantro and green onion to a large mixing bowl. Once cool, add the millet and toss to combine. Pour the Thai Peanut Sauce atop the millet/vegetable mixture and stir to thoroughly coat. Sprinkle the peanuts on top of the salad and chill until ready to serve.

Vegan Taco Salad

Nut-free, soy-free, gluten-free
Splurge: Top each salad with diced avocado or Vegan Sour Cream (page 167)
Serves 4 • 30 minutes to prepare

━ ● ━

Long before burrito bowls and sushi salads were popular, there was the taco salad: the original gangster of deconstructed food. In this recipe, we give the tried and true taco salad a plant-based makeover with hearty, spicy lentils and plenty of veggies. For the taco seasoning, you can either buy a packet at the grocery store or make your own at home with spices like chili powder, cumin and paprika. If you're feeling fancy, you can also whip up a batch of our Vegan Sour Cream (page 167) to take this taco salad to the next level.

1 cup (201 g) brown or green lentils, rinsed

2 tbsp (15 g) taco seasoning

4 cups (188 g) shredded lettuce

1 cup (201 g) black beans, drained and rinsed

2 cups (288 g) corn, drained

1 cup (149 g) cherry tomatoes, halved

½ cup (80 g) salsa or pico de gallo

1 tbsp (15 ml) olive oil

1 lime, juiced

Cilantro and green onion, optional

Avocado and Vegan Sour Cream (page 167), for serving, optional

Cook the lentils according to package directions. Drain excess water and transfer the cooked lentils to a large mixing bowl. Add the taco seasoning and stir to thoroughly combine, gently smashing some of the lentils with the back of a fork. Adjust seasonings to taste.

To assemble, divide the lettuce, black beans, corn, tomatoes, salsa and lentil taco "meat" among 4 bowls. Drizzle each with a touch of olive oil and lime juice. Garnish with cilantro, green onion, avocado and Vegan Sour Cream, if desired.

Cucumber, Tomato and White Bean Salad

Nut-free, soy-free, gluten-free
Splurge: Add olives or just about any fresh herb such as dill, mint, oregano, tarragon or basil
Serves 4–6 • 15 minutes to prepare

This salad is our go-to for a summer lunch or potluck. Quick and easy to assemble, the flavor improves if you let it sit refrigerated for an hour or so. If you haven't seeded a cucumber before, slice it in half the long way. Then take a small spoon and scrape out the seeds. We also like to do a striped half-peel, mostly for dramatic effect.

2 large tomatoes, seeded (about 1 lb [454 g])

1 large cucumber, seeded and cut in ½-inch (13-mm) pieces

1 (15½-oz [440-g]) can white beans, rinsed and drained

1 tbsp (15 ml) rice vinegar

1 tbsp (15 ml) olive oil

Salt and pepper

Olives and fresh herbs, for serving, optional

Add all of the ingredients to a large bowl. Stir gently. Add salt and pepper to taste.

Chilled Soba Noodle Salad

Nut-free, gluten-free
Splurge: none
Serves 2—3 • 25 minutes to prepare

⚫

Ramen, meet your match! There's a new Japanese noodle in town, and it packs way more fiber and protein than its microwavable cousin. You can find soba noodles pretty easily in the Asian section of most grocery stores. If you're gluten-free, be sure to look for a brand that makes its soba noodles from 100 percent buckwheat. Many packaged varieties use a blend that includes wheat flour, so read the ingredients carefully before you hit the checkout line.

6 oz (170 g) soba noodles

1 carrot, peeled

½ cucumber, thinly sliced

3 green onions, sliced diagonally

2 cups (681 g) purple cabbage, shredded

1 tbsp (10 g) sesame seeds

¼ cup (60 ml) Sesame Salad Dressing (page 168)

Cook the soba noodles according to package directions. Drain, rinse with cold water and set aside to cool. Use a vegetable peeler to create long, thin ribbons of carrot and add them to a large mixing bowl. Then toss in the cucumber, green onion and purple cabbage. Add the soba noodles and sesame seeds to the vegetables and toss to combine. Pour the Sesame Salad Dressing atop the salad and stir to thoroughly coat. Set in the refrigerator to chill until ready to serve.

Warm Wild Rice Salad with Mushrooms and Arugula

Nut-free, soy-free, gluten-free
Splurge: Add toasted chopped pecans or roasted butternut squash
Serves 4 • 60 minutes to prepare

━ • ◄

Here's a little wild rice trivia for you: Wild rice is actually a seed and not a grain at all. And like most seeds, it's a nutritional powerhouse, packed with protein, fiber and loads of other good things. If you have a little extra time and it just so happens to be fall, make it deluxe with a little roasted butternut squash.

1 tbsp (15 ml) olive oil, divided

1 small onion, diced small

1 cup (144 g) wild rice mix

1¾ cups (414 ml) water

1 tsp thyme

1 bay leaf

¼ cup (38 g) raisins

8 oz (227 g) white mushrooms, sliced

1 cup (40 g) arugula

1 tbsp (15 ml) balsamic vinegar

Toasted pecans and roasted butternut squash, optional

Salt and pepper

Heat ½ of the olive oil in a medium saucepan over medium heat. Add the onion and cook until soft, 8 to 10 minutes.

Add the rice. Cook for a few minutes and add water, thyme and bay leaf. Bring to a boil, lower the heat to a soft simmer, cover and cook for 45 minutes. Remove from the heat, quickly take the lid off to add the raisins and then let the rice sit and steam covered for another 15 minutes.

In the meantime, sauté the mushrooms in the remaining ½ tablespoon (7 ml) of olive oil until slightly browned and soft, 10 minutes.

Mix the rice and mushrooms together and remove the bay leaf. Add the arugula, balsamic vinegar, toasted pecans and roasted butternut squash, then salt and pepper to taste.

Kale Salad with Cherries and Almonds

Soy-free, gluten-free
Splurge: Add blueberries and 8 oz (227 g) grilled tofu
Serves 4 • 30 minutes to prepare

➤ • ◄

The colors in this salad are fit for the holidays, but your best bet is to make it at the tail end of summer when kale and cherries are both in season. When each ingredient is at its peak of freshness, the entire meal just tastes so much better. Not to mention, shopping seasonally can save you a pretty penny at the supermarket. Be sure to use French lentils for this recipe, rather than ordinary ones. They hold their shape better when cooked and pack 9 grams of protein per serving!

1 cup (201 g) French lentils

4 cups (946 ml) water

8 cups (536 g) kale, chopped

2 tsp (10 ml) olive oil

2 cups (308 g) cherries, halved

2 cups (300 g) blueberries, optional

⅓ cup (78 ml) Simple Vinaigrette (page 158)

½ cup (46 g) almonds, sliced

Grilled tofu, optional

Thoroughly rinse the lentils in a colander to remove any debris. Then, combine the lentils and water in a saucepan. Bring to a boil, then reduce heat and simmer for about 20 minutes, or until the lentils are tender. When they're done cooking, drain the lentils and set them aside to cool.

Meanwhile, put the kale in a serving bowl and add the olive oil. Massage the oil into the kale leaves until they're dark green and softened a bit. Then add the cherries, blueberries and Simple Vinaigrette. Toss gently to combine.

To serve, place a scoop of lentils in the bottom of each salad bowl. Add the dressed kale, cherries and blueberries. Top with sliced almonds and grilled tofu, if desired. Serve immediately.

Rustic Market Salad

Soy-free, gluten-free
Splurge: Substitute dried currants for raisins
Serves 2 • 60 minutes to prepare

— • —

This recipe combines some very inexpensive, ordinary ingredients into something delightful and easy to prepare. Bonus points: It keeps perfectly if you're taking your lunch to work. So next time you're making up some rice and lentils, set aside a little extra and you can pull this salad together in no time.

Serve with the Orange Chia Dressing (page 162) or Simple Vinaigrette (page 158).

½ cup (105 g) brown rice

½ cup (100 g) green lentils

2 large carrots, cut on the bias (or just plain sliced)

2 radishes, sliced thin

2 ribs celery, sliced thin

¼ cup (38 g) raisins

¼ cup (30 g) walnuts, chopped

4 cups (160 g) mixed greens, washed and dried

Cook the rice and lentils according to package directions. While the rice and lentils are cooking, prep the rest of your ingredients.

Set aside the rice and lentils to cool. Assemble all the ingredients in a large bowl, toss and serve.

CHAPTER 5

Slurp Worthy Soups

Soups, stews and chilis are the workhorses of your budget vegan diet. Not only are they rich in nutrients and easy to prepare, a single batch makes multiple servings to enjoy throughout the week. Soups, stews and chilis also freeze really well, so anything leftover can be packed in containers and tucked into the freezer until you're ready to have it again.

One of the most important considerations in preparing any soup is the stock or broth. Many of the vegetable stocks you find at the store can be a little bitter, while broths are often far too salty. Try several until you find one you like. When your favorite goes on sale, stock up! Stocks and broth keep for a very long time and they're always good to have on hand.

If you prefer going the DIY route, we also have an excellent recipe for making your own Easy Vegetable Broth (page 107), which uses affordable ingredients and bits and pieces you probably would have tossed or composted anyhow. It's the perfect little project for a rainy afternoon.

Lentil Soup with Greens

Gluten-free, soy-free, nut-free
Splurge: French green lentils
Serves 6 • 60 minutes, mostly hands off

- • -

We really prefer a lentil soup to just about any other. It's hearty, satisfying and so easy to prepare. This recipe calls for a basic green lentil, but if you feel like a splurge, go with French green lentils. They tend to hold their shape far better than their fellow lentils, but also happen to be ever so slightly more expensive than regular green lentils (about $0.40 per pound). You can also substitute any hearty green (kale, collards) for the chard. If you prefer soup with a smoother, creamier consistency, purée just enough of the soup to add thickness, about 1 cup (240 ml), before adding the chard.

3 tbsp (45 ml) extra-virgin olive oil

2 cups (300 g) onion, diced

1 cup (100 g) celery, diced

1 cup (130 g) carrots, diced

2 garlic cloves, minced

4 cups (946 ml) vegetable broth

1¼ cups (250 g) green lentils, rinsed and drained

1 (15-oz [425-g]) can crushed tomatoes (use diced if you prefer a chunkier soup)

1 bunch chard, de-stemmed and chopped

Salt and pepper

Heat the olive oil in large, heavy saucepan over medium-high heat. Add the onions, celery, carrots and garlic; sauté until the vegetables are soft and barely browned, about 15 minutes. Add the vegetable broth, lentils and tomatoes with their juices and bring to boil. Reduce heat to medium-low, cover and simmer until the lentils are tender, about 35 minutes.

Add the chard and cook another 5 to 7 minutes. Season with salt and pepper and serve.

Roasted Carrot Curried Soup

Nut-free, soy-free, gluten-free
Splurge: Top with fresh cilantro
Serves 6 · 60 minutes to prepare

＞ ● ＜

This soup is perfection in the fall—from color to flavor, it exudes warmth. The basic preparation is so simple, but it dresses up beautifully with a few fresh herbs or homemade croutons.

2 tsp (5 g) curry powder

1 tsp kosher salt

2 tbsp (30 ml) extra-virgin olive oil

1½ lb (680 g) medium carrots, trimmed, peeled, sliced lengthwise and cut into 1-inch (25-mm) pieces

2 medium yellow onions, quartered and sliced in 1-inch (25-mm) chunks

1 (15-oz [425-g]) can full-fat coconut milk

2 cups (470 ml) water or broth

Half a lemon, juiced

Fresh cilantro, for serving, optional

Preheat the oven to 400°F (204°C).

Mix the curry powder, salt and olive oil together in the bottom of a large bowl. Add the carrots and onions to the bowl. Toss to coat, and then pour it all out onto a parchment-lined baking sheet.

Bake until the vegetables are very tender and just beginning to caramelize, about 30 to 40 minutes.

Remove the vegetables from the oven and transfer them to a large pot. Add coconut milk and water (or broth). Let the mixture simmer for just a few minutes. Then, working in batches, transfer to a blender and blend until smooth.

Return the soup to the pot and warm. Add lemon juice and fresh cilantro before serving.

Watermelon Gazpacho

Nut-free, soy-free
Splurge: Garnish with fresh basil or mint leaves
Serves 2 • 15 minutes to prepare

— • ◂

Eating nothing but cold salads during the summer can get boring really fast. Why not switch up your lunchtime routine with a chilled soup? Gazpacho originated in the southern Spanish region of Andalusia and is commonly eaten during the hottest months of the year as a way to keep cool. In this recipe, searing the watermelon before blending it into a creamy soup provides a hint of extra flavor. However, you can also just toss cubed watermelon into a blender with the other ingredients and purée away. If you're feeling fancy, garnish each bowl with some fresh basil or mint leaves.

4 cups (615 g) watermelon

1 tsp olive oil

½ cup (80 g) tomatoes, diced

½ cup (75 g) cucumber, diced

½ jalapeño pepper, seeded

1 garlic clove, smashed

1 tbsp (15 ml) olive oil

1 tbsp (15 ml) lime juice

½ tbsp (7 ml) balsamic vinegar

Salt, to taste

Black pepper, to taste

Fresh basil or mint leaves, for serving, optional

Slice the watermelon into ½-inch (13-mm) thick pieces and remove the rind. Blot excess moisture with a paper towel. Heat a pan coated with the olive oil over medium-high heat for a few minutes.

Place the slices of watermelon in the pan and sear for 2 minutes on each side or until they begin to caramelize. Remove from heat and set aside to cool.

Once the watermelon is cool, place all the ingredients in a blender and blend until smooth. Serve immediately at room temperature, or chill in the fridge for 1 to 2 hours before serving. Garnish with fresh basil or mint leaves, if desired.

Chickpea Curry

Nut-free, soy-free, gluten-free
Splurge: Add 1 (14-oz [396-g]) can of culinary (full-fat!) coconut milk before serving
Serves 4–6 • 30 minutes to prepare

▬ ● ▬

We love, love, love all of the curries. We could eat it every day. And if not curry, then Mexican. Mexican food is pretty awesome, too. But back to curries. One-pot curries are always a quick, healthy and easy dinner option to master. Experiment with different curry varieties and brands until you find one you're really into. This chickpea curry is fabulous on its own, but you can also serve it over rice or with a side of steamed kale to make it a heartier meal.

1 tbsp (15 ml) olive oil

1 medium onion, diced small

2 cloves of garlic, minced

2 tbsp (15 g) curry powder

1 bay leaf

1 head cauliflower florets, cut in pieces

3 medium red potatoes, cut in ½-inch (13-mm) chunks

1 (15-oz [425-g]) can crushed tomatoes

1 (15-oz [425-g]) can chickpeas, rinsed and drained

2 cups (473 ml) vegetable stock (or water)

1 cup (160 g) frozen peas

Coconut milk, optional

Salt and pepper

Heat the olive oil in a Dutch oven or medium saucepan over medium heat. Add the onion and cook until very soft and just starting to brown, about 12 to 15 minutes. Add the garlic and cook for about a minute before adding the curry and bay leaf. Cook for another 30 seconds. Then add the cauliflower, potatoes, crushed tomatoes, chickpeas and vegetable stock.

Bring to a simmer, lower the heat and continue to simmer gently for about 20 minutes or until the potatoes are just tender.

Add the peas and coconut milk, if you're using it, and cook just another minute. Remove the bay leaf and add salt and pepper to taste.

Roasted Tomato and Garlic Soup

Nut-free, soy-free, gluten-free
Splurge: Add ½ cup (20 g) fresh chopped basil at the end of cooking
Serves 4 • 70 minutes to prepare

● ● ◄

What do you do when tomatoes are on mega-sale, and you get overzealous and buy too many? Make soup, of course! This is a great recipe to make from tomatoes that are too squishy or bruised to slice up for sandwiches. It makes for an ideal lunch when paired with a salad, or a satisfying dinner partnered with a warm panini or vegan grilled cheese. The roasted tomatoes and garlic provide plenty of flavor, but the addition of fresh basil really kicks it up a notch.

2½ lb (1 kg) ripe tomatoes, cored and quartered

8 cloves garlic, unpeeled

¼ cup (60 ml) olive oil

3 cups (710 ml) vegetable broth

2 bay leaves

3 tbsp (43 g) vegan butter

1 tsp salt

½ tsp black pepper

Fresh basil, optional

Preheat the oven to 400°F (204°C).

Combine the tomatoes and garlic on a baking sheet lined with parchment paper and drizzle with olive oil. Roast for 35 minutes, or until the tomatoes are caramelized.

Once the garlic is cool enough to handle, peel the cloves and transfer them to a large stockpot along with the tomatoes and their juices. Turn to medium heat. Add the vegetable broth, bay leaves, vegan butter, salt and pepper. Bring the mixture to a boil, and then reduce to a simmer. Cook for 20 minutes or until the liquid has reduced by about a third. Stir in the basil, if using. Discard the bay leaf.

Transfer the soup to a blender and purée until smooth, working in batches if necessary. Return the soup to the stockpot and warm over low heat. Adjust salt and pepper to taste. Serve hot.

★ Black Bean and Tempeh Chili

Nut-free

Splurge: Top with fresh avocado, cilantro and diced tomatoes

Serves 6 · 40 minutes to prepare

— • • ◂

Adding tempeh to chili makes this recipe a protein powerhouse. Yep, a powerhouse. In my world, chili needs a little extra color, so I always like to add frozen corn, but I understand this is a point of contention in many households. So I leave the corn as optional. No need to upset the 'purists' with a little splash of color. And if you're not a fan of tempeh, you can easily swap it out for a third can of beans.

If you want to use dried beans to make this recipe, dried beans typically double in volume (and weight for that matter). So you'll want to soak ¾ cup (150 g) dried black beans and ¾ cup (150 g) dried kidney beans. —Katie

¼ cup (60 ml) olive oil, divided

1 (8-oz [227-g]) package tempeh, crumbled

2 cups (302 g) chopped onions

1 medium red bell pepper, coarsely chopped

4 garlic cloves, chopped

2 tbsp (15 g) chili powder

2 tsp (1 g) dried oregano

1½ tsp (4 g) ground cumin

½ tsp cayenne pepper

1 (15-oz [425-g]) can black beans, drained, ½ cup (120 ml) liquid reserved

1 (15-oz [425-g]) can kidney beans

1 (15-oz [425-g]) can diced fire-roasted tomatoes

1 cup (240 ml) water

1 cup (145 g) frozen corn, optional

Salt and pepper

Avocado, cilantro and diced tomatoes, for serving, optional

Heat 1 tablespoon (15 ml) of olive oil in heavy large pot over medium-high heat. Add crumbled tempeh and cook until just browned, 6 to 8 minutes. Remove the tempeh from pan and set aside.

Heat the remaining 3 tablespoons (45 ml) of olive oil in a heavy large pot over medium-high heat. Add the onions, bell peppers, and garlic; sauté until the onions soften, about 10 minutes. Mix in the chili powder, oregano, cumin and cayenne; stir for 2 minutes.

Mix in the beans, ½ cup (120 ml) reserved bean liquid, tomatoes, water, tempeh and corn (if using). Bring the chili to boil, stirring occasionally. Reduce heat to medium-low and simmer until the flavors blend and the chili thickens, stirring occasionally, about 15 minutes. Season to taste with salt and pepper and top with avocado, cilantro and diced tomatoes.

Minestrone Soup

Nut-free, soy-free
Splurge: Fresh parsley or basil
Serves 6 · 40 minutes to prepare

➤ ● ◄

The minestrone foundation is simple: a light tomato soup with pasta, vegetables and beans. It's adaptable to any season and just about anything languishing in your refrigerator. In the winter, my minestrones are more substantial and often include hearty greens and butternut squash, while in summer they tend to be packed with squash, zucchini and green beans from the garden. It's the ideal recipe for cleaning out your refrigerator.
—Katie

1 tbsp (15 ml) olive oil

1 onion, diced

2 carrots, chopped

2 stalks celery, chopped

3 cloves garlic, minced

1 tsp dried oregano

1 tsp dried basil

1 (15-oz [425-g]) can diced tomatoes

4 cups (946 ml) vegetable stock or water

1 large zucchini, diced

¾ cup (135 g) frozen spinach

1 (15-oz [425-g]) can kidney beans, rinsed and drained

½ cup (58 g) dried pasta, cooked

Salt and pepper

Fresh parsley or basil, for serving, optional

Heat the olive oil in a large Dutch oven or soup pot over medium heat. Add the onion, carrots and celery. Cook until soft, about 10 minutes. Add the garlic, cooking another minute before adding the oregano and basil.

Add the diced tomatoes, vegetable stock (or water), zucchini and spinach. Simmer for 10 minutes or until the zucchini just starts to soften. Add the beans and pasta and cook gently for another 5 minutes. Season with salt and pepper to taste and top with optional fresh parsley or basil.

TIP: I prefer to cook my pasta separately to keep the soup from getting too starchy, but if you're short on time, toss the pasta in when you add the zucchini.

Roasted Cauliflower Soup with Lemon Parsley Pesto and Croutons

Nut-free, soy-free
Splurge: none
Serves 6 • 60 minutes to prepare

— • ◄

Lemon parsley pesto brings the perfect pop of color and flavor to this simple (and incredibly inexpensive) soup. If you're short on time, you can easily skip the croutons and still have a stellar soup.

1 head cauliflower, roughly cut into 2-inch (50-mm) pieces (about 8 cups [1.8 kg])

2 tbsp (30 ml) olive oil, divided

2 medium yellow onions, halved and sliced thin (about 3 cups [400 g])

½ tsp thyme

5 cups (1.2 L) vegetable broth

CROUTONS

½ baguette, cut in ½-inch (13-mm) cubes

1 tsp olive oil

Salt and pepper

LEMON PARSLEY PESTO

1 bunch flat-leaf parsley (about 1 cup [40 g]), stems removed

1 lemon, zest and juice (about 2 tbsp [20 g])

4 tbsp (60 ml) olive oil

Preheat the oven to 425°F (218°C). Line a baking sheet with parchment paper.

Toss the cauliflower in 1 tablespoon (15 ml) of olive oil. Pour out onto a lined baking sheet. Bake for 30 minutes or until just lightly browned and soft. Set aside the parchment-lined baking sheet to use for the croutons.

When the cauliflower has been in the oven for about 20 minutes, you can start cooking the onions. Heat 1 tablespoon (15 ml) of olive oil over medium heat in a large Dutch oven or soup pot. Add the onion and cook for about 10 minutes, or until the onions are very soft but not browned. Add the thyme, vegetable broth and roasted cauliflower.

Bring to a boil, reduce heat and simmer for 15 minutes.

Working in small batches, transfer the soup to a blender and blend until smooth or at desired smoothness. I like to keep mine a little on the chunky side.

In the meantime, toss the baguette in 1 teaspoon of olive oil and add a little salt and pepper. Bake at 425°F (218°C) for 5 minutes; toss and bake another 2 to 3 minutes until just barely browned.

To make the pesto, add the parsley, lemon juice and olive oil to the small bowl of a food processor. Blend until smooth. Drizzle the soup with pesto, top with croutons and serve.

Miso Greens Soup

Nut-free
Splurge: Top with sliced avocado
Serves 2 • 15 minutes to prepare

— • —

This soup is a necessity during the holiday season—the perfect detox from all of the rich holiday foods. Added bonus: It's ridiculously quick and easy to make. Keep in mind that boiling miso kills all the good digestive helpers it contains. For this reason, this soup doesn't reheat that well, but the recipe halves easily if you want to avoid any waste.

4 cups (946 ml) water

2–3 leaves kale, ribbed and sliced thin

1 cup (150 g) snow peas

½ (12-oz [340-g]) package firm silken tofu, cut in ½-inch (13-mm) cubes

4 tbsp (55 g) white or yellow miso paste

2 green onions, sliced thin

Avocado, for serving, optional

Bring water to a boil. Add the kale and snow peas. Cook for about a minute, reduce heat and add the tofu.

In a separate bowl, mix the miso and 4 tablespoons (60 ml) of soup water to make a paste. Add to the soup, along with the green onions and optional avocado. Serve immediately.

TIP: If you want to make this a touch heartier, you can add ¼ cup (30 g) of orzo pasta. Just be sure to give the pasta a head start before adding the vegetables.

Mulligatawny Soup

Nut-free, soy-free, gluten-free
Splurge: Add in extra vegetables or cubed tofu
Serves 6 • 45 minutes to prepare

• ▪ ◂

Whenever I start with a recipe that has spices I don't already have in my kitchen, I go straight for the bulk bins. Buy just what you need for a few cents, rather than investing in an entire bottle, sure to go flat before it's used up. Yes, I'm looking at you, garam masala. Serve with rice. —Katie

¼ cup (60 ml) vegetable oil

2 medium onions, diced

5 cloves garlic, minced

1½ tbsp (12 g) garam masala

1½ tsp (4 g) ground coriander

1 tsp turmeric

½ tsp cayenne pepper

1 bay leaf

2 cups (400 g) dried red lentils

1 cup (128 g) carrots, chopped

2 medium red potatoes, cut in ½-inch (13-mm) chunks

8 cups (1.8 L) vegetable broth or water

1 cup (240 ml) canned, unsweetened coconut milk

3 tbsp (45 ml) fresh lemon juice

Tofu, for serving, optional

Salt and pepper

Heat the vegetable oil in a large pot over medium-high heat. Add the onions and cook until golden brown, 16 to 18 minutes, stirring often. Add the garlic and cook for a minute. Add the garam masala, coriander, turmeric, cayenne and bay leaf. Continue to cook another minute.

Add the lentils, carrots and potatoes; stir until coated. Add vegetable broth or water. Bring the soup to a boil; reduce heat to medium and simmer until the lentils are very tender, about 20 minutes. Discard the bay leaf.

Working in batches, purée the soup in a blender until smooth. Return to the pot. Stir in the coconut milk, lemon juice and optional tofu. Season to taste with salt and pepper. Serve over rice.

Easy Vegetable Broth

Nut-free, soy-free, gluten-free
Splurge: none
Makes 4–6 cups (946–1,420 ml) • 90 minutes to prepare, mostly hands off

➤ ● ◄

Vegetable broth is one of those things I always avoided making. It felt like a lifestyle I didn't want to take on, along with making my own pine needle baskets and darning socks. Then one day, I was staring at a pile of leftover vegetables and decided to test the waters. To my surprise, it was fairly effortless and the results far superior to anything store-bought. And to top it off, it freezes really well. I recommend getting a set of freezer containers, like Tupperware, in a variety of volumes (¼ cup [60 ml], ½ cup [120 ml], 1 cup [240 ml]) for easy storing and defrosting.

When making broth you can add all sorts of leftover veggies, but avoid onion skins, broccoli, cauliflower and tomatoes. Those all have the potential to make your broth bitter. Do add leftover mushroom stems, potato skins, corn and most other things. —Katie

2 tbsp (30 ml) olive oil

2 onions, roughly chopped

2 carrots, roughly chopped

5 stalks celery, roughly chopped

6 cups (1.4 L) water

1 bunch parsley

¼ cup (50 g) green lentils, picked through for debris and rinsed

1 bay leaf

2 tsp (10 g) salt

½ tsp thyme

4 cloves garlic

Heat the olive oil in a large stockpot over medium heat. Add the onions, carrots and celery. Cook for 10 minutes or until soft.

Add the remaining ingredients and water. Cook for about an hour. Strain the liquid from the solids. You can use cheesecloth if you want to get fancy, but I usually settle for a fine mesh strainer and call it good.

Transfer the broth to storage containers to freeze or refrigerate until you're ready to use.

Mornings

They say breakfast is the most important meal of the day. We couldn't agree more, unless brunch is an option. In that case, we're hitting the snooze button and mixing up some mimosas. Whether you're enjoying a lazy Sunday morning at home or dashing out the door for work, there are so many delicious ways you can start your day with a healthy, plant-based meal.

On the following pages, you'll find budget-friendly breakfast and brunch dishes that will please even the pickiest eaters. Kids go crazy for our Pancakes with Roasted Bananas (page 110), while prep-ahead breakfasts like our Zucchini Banana Bread Muffins (page 125) and Pineapple Scones (page 114) provide options for vegans on-the-go. No matter what your morning looks like, there's always time to squeeze in a healthy bite.

Pancakes with Roasted Bananas

Nut-free, soy-free
Splurge: Serve with coconut oil, peanut butter and/or pure maple syrup
Serves 4 • 30 minutes to prepare

● • ◄

If you haven't made these before, you're in for a treat. Roasted bananas take just a few extra minutes to prepare, but are entirely worth the effort. Firm, even slightly under-ripe, bananas work great for this recipe as they soften quite a bit as they cook. We suggest using maple/agave-blend syrup, because it's less expensive than pure maple syrup.

2–3 bananas, cut into ½-inch (13-mm) pieces

3 tbsp (45 ml) maple/agave-blend syrup

¼ tsp cinnamon

1 cup (125 g) unbleached all-purpose flour (or half all-purpose and half whole wheat)

2 tbsp (23 g) baking powder

½ tsp cinnamon

1 tbsp (12 g) sugar

⅛ tsp salt

1 cup (240 ml) nondairy milk

2 tbsp (30 ml) vegetable oil

Coconut oil, peanut butter and pure maple syrup, for serving, optional

Preheat the oven to 375°F (191°C).

Place the sliced bananas on a baking sheet lined with parchment paper. Drizzle the maple/agave-blend syrup over the banana pieces and toss to evenly coat. Sprinkle bananas with cinnamon and bake for 10 to 15 minutes, or until the pieces are soft and sticky. Set aside.

While the bananas are baking, combine the flour, baking powder, cinnamon, sugar and salt in a bowl. In a separate bowl, combine the milk and oil. Add the milk mixture to the flour mixture and stir just until moistened; a few lumps are okay (don't overmix or the pancakes will be tough).

Heat a nonstick pan over medium heat (you can add some oil, but with a nonstick pan you shouldn't need it.) Give the batter a quick stir and maybe another splash of nondairy milk so it's nice and pourable before adding it to the pan. Then pour the batter onto the pan to form circles about 6 inches (15 cm) in diameter. Cook the pancakes for a couple of minutes on one side, until bubbles appear on the surface. Flip the pancakes and cook the other side until golden brown, about 3 minutes.

Serve the pancakes topped with roasted bananas and maple/agave-blend syrup or other additional toppings if desired.

Sweet Potato Breakfast Boats

Nut-free, soy-free, gluten-free
Splurge: none
Serves 2 • 20 minutes to prepare

◗ ● ◖

Sweet potatoes are a delicious and versatile, yet often overlooked, breakfast food. They can stand in for toast when sliced thin, cooked on a cast-iron skillet and topped with avocado, and they offer a healthier way to do hash browns. Here, we make them into boats we can fill with our favorite toppings. We went with a Southwest theme for this recipe, but you can really use anything you have sitting in your pantry or fridge. Chickpeas, broccoli, bell pepper, spinach—get creative!

1 sweet potato

½ avocado, mashed

⅛ tsp cumin

⅛ tsp cayenne pepper

½ cup (100 g) black beans, drained and rinsed

½ cup (72 g) frozen corn, thawed

¼ cup (65 g) salsa

Salt and pepper

Using a fork, poke holes all around the sweet potato. Place it on a paper towel or microwave-safe plate and microwave for 8 to 10 minutes, or until cooked through.

Cut the sweet potato in half lengthwise, and then, with the fleshy parts facing up, cut a slit lengthwise down the middle of each half. Use a couple of forks to split open the sweet potato halves so you're left with little pockets.

In a small bowl, mash the avocado with the cumin and cayenne. Then, fill each sweet-potato boat with the avocado, followed by the black beans, corn and salsa. Season with salt and pepper to taste.

Pineapple Scones

Soy-free
Splurge: none
Makes 8–10 scones • 30 minutes to prepare

◗ ● ◖

When it comes to breakfast goodies, I've always been more of a muffin or bagel person. Not to mention—I've never considered myself a baker. Oh, how things have changed. While I used to scoff at scones for their crumbly texture and lack of sweetness, I've really come to adore them. The recipe below is easy to make and fun to eat. Getting a surprise chunk of pineapple in each bite adds the perfect jolt of sweetness! —Kate

3 cups (390 g) whole wheat flour

1 tbsp (12 g) baking powder

1 tsp baking soda

½ tsp salt

¾ tsp lemon juice

¾ cup (177 ml) nondairy milk

3 tbsp (45 ml) maple syrup

¼ cup and 2 tbsp (82 g) coconut oil, frozen

1 tsp vanilla extract

1 (8-oz [227-g]) can crushed pineapple, drained

Cooking spray

1 tbsp (9 g) coconut sugar (or brown sugar)

2 tbsp (11 g) sliced raw almonds

1 tbsp (3 g) fresh rosemary, finely chopped

Preheat the oven to 425°F (218°C).

Sift together the flour, baking powder, baking soda and salt in a large mixing bowl. In a separate bowl, combine the lemon juice and nondairy milk. Once the mixture curdles, add the maple syrup.

Remove the coconut oil from the freezer and cut it into small pieces. Work the coconut oil pieces into the dry mix until fully incorporated. Be careful not to handle it too much, though. You don't want the coconut oil to melt until it gets into the oven! Slowly pour the curdled milk mixture into the dry ingredients a little at a time, followed by the vanilla and pineapple. Stir until all of the ingredients are fully combined.

Carefully transfer the dough to a floured surface and form it into a ball. Use your hands to flatten it into a 2-inch (5-cm)-thick slab. Fold the dough in half by picking up the end furthest from you and bringing it down to meet the end closest to you. Flatten it a bit, and then fold the dough in half again from left to right. Use a rolling pin to roll the dough into a 1½-inch (4-cm) slab. With a drinking glass, stamp the dough into circles (or use a knife to cut triangles) and transfer to a baking sheet lined with parchment paper. Take the remaining dough and repeat the fold, fold, roll and cut process. You should end up with between 8 and 10 scones.

Lightly spray the tops of the scones with olive oil or coconut oil cooking spray. Sprinkle each with coconut sugar, and top with sliced almonds and rosemary. Bake for 10 minutes or until the scones are fluffy and golden brown. Transfer the scones to a wire rack and allow them to cool slightly before serving.

Crispy Vegan Bacon

Nut-free, gluten-free
Splurge: none
Serves 4 • 30 minutes to prepare

— • • —

Who knew rice paper was good for more than making spring rolls? You'll be stunned by how it mimics the flavor and texture of bacon when marinated and baked to crispy perfection. The key is in the marinade. Before anything else, you'll first soak the rice paper in a bath of soy sauce or tamari, brown sugar, apple cider vinegar and a touch of liquid smoke to give it that salty, savory taste you love. You can even add a splash of bourbon if you're feeling adventurous! Once you pop your bacon in the oven, keep a close eye on it. Your breakfast can go from crispy to burnt within a few seconds.

2 tbsp (30 ml) soy sauce or tamari

1 tbsp (15 ml) apple cider vinegar

1 tbsp (9 g) nutritional yeast

1 tbsp (15 ml) canola oil

1 tsp liquid smoke

2 tsp (9 g) brown sugar

½ tsp bourbon, optional

4 sheets of rice paper

Preheat the oven to 375°F (191°C) and line two baking sheets with parchment paper. Make the marinade by whisking together the soy sauce or tamari, apple cider vinegar, nutritional yeast, canola oil, liquid smoke, brown sugar and bourbon, if using, in a small mixing bowl. Fill a second mixing bowl with water, and set both dishes aside.

Stack two pieces of rice paper on top of one another and cut them into 1½-inch (4-cm) strips using kitchen scissors. This should yield about six strips. Holding two strips of rice paper together, dip them in the water and press them together until they stick. Then, dip that double-rice-paper strip into the marinade. Swish it around and give it a good soak. Lay the marinated rice paper on the baking sheet. Repeat with the remaining five pairs of rice paper strips until the baking sheet is full. Repeat the entire process with two more pieces of rice paper to fill the second baking sheet.

Bake the rice paper for 8 to 10 minutes, until golden and crispy, but not burnt. Remove from the oven and cool on a wire rack before eating. You'll have quite a bit of marinade left over, so you can repeat the entire cutting, soaking, marinating and baking process to yield double the amount of crispy vegan bacon. Once cool, serve immediately with our Tofu Scrambled Eggs (page 124) or on our BLT with Sriracha Mayo (page 159). You can also store it in an airtight container in the fridge for up to three days, but it's best eaten fresh.

Apple Cinnamon Oatmeal

Nut-free, soy-free, gluten-free
Splurge: Top oatmeal with chopped almonds or pecans
Serves 2 • 10 minutes to prepare

— ● —

You know those mornings when you wake up and you can smell autumn in the air? Yeah, that's when you're going to want to make this oatmeal. Apples are cheapest when they're in season, which typically starts in September and runs through the end of the year. You can use any type of apple with this recipe, but our absolute favorite is Honeycrisp. If you're short on time, you can zap your oatmeal in the microwave for three to four minutes before you dash out the door.

1 cup (80 g) rolled oats

1 tsp cinnamon

2 cups (470 ml) water

2 medium apples, diced, divided

2 tbsp (30 ml) maple/agave-blend syrup, optional

Chopped almonds or pecans, for serving, optional

Combine the rolled oats, cinnamon, water and half of the apple pieces in a saucepan and heat over medium-low. Bring to a simmer, stirring frequently. Continue to cook until the oats reach your desired consistency and the apples are soft, 8 to 10 minutes. Transfer the oatmeal to a bowl and stir in the remaining apple pieces. Drizzle with the maple/agave-blend syrup, dust with additional cinnamon and top with chopped almonds or pecans, if desired. Serve warm.

Peanut Butter and Jelly Granola

Soy-free, gluten-free
Splurge: Add in chopped peanuts, chocolate chips, dried bananas, sunflower seeds or hemp seeds
Serves 4–6 • 30 minutes to prepare

⬤ ● ◀

This granola is a breakfast favorite around our house, sprinkled over a bowl of vanilla (nondairy) yogurt with a few slices of banana and maybe even a dollop of jam to make it extra jelly. Because some mornings you just need things to be a little extra jelly. —Katie

3 tbsp (34 g) peanut butter

3 tbsp (45 ml) agave

1 tbsp (15 ml) water

1 tsp vanilla

2 cups (160 g) oats

½ tsp cinnamon

½ cup (75 g) raisins

Chopped peanuts, chocolate chips, dried bananas, sunflower seeds or hemp seeds, optional

Preheat the oven to 325°F (163°C). Line a baking sheet with parchment paper.

Combine the peanut butter, agave and water in a microwave-safe bowl or coffee mug. Coffee mugs are nice, because they have a handle. Warm the peanut butter mixture in the microwave on high power for 20 seconds and stir. Microwave for another 20 seconds or until nice and melty. Stir well, add the vanilla and set aside.

Combine the oats and cinnamon in a large bowl. Drizzle the wet ingredients over the dry and mix well. Spread evenly on a baking sheet and cook for 10 minutes. Stir and return to the oven for another 10 minutes, or until the oats just start to brown.

Let the granola cool completely. Mix in raisins and other optional ingredients and store in an airtight container.

Biscuits and Gravy

Nut-free

Splurge: Add fresh herbs like thyme or rosemary to the gravy with the salt and pepper

Serves 4 · 40 minutes to prepare

● ● ◄

Here's an interesting fact: Several brands of those store-bought biscuits in a can are vegan. So if you're not up for some biscuit prep, grab a can. But if you are (they're pretty easy), know that your efforts are best spent making a lot. Any uncooked biscuits can be frozen for later. Just remember not to defrost them before baking and bake for a few minutes longer than you usually would.

The secret to making good biscuits is keeping all your ingredients cold, ice cold. By nature, vegan butters are softer than real butter, so we always cut our butter into ½-inch (13-mm) cubes and pop them in the freezer for about twenty minutes before we start working. If you can find vegan butter in sticks, it makes measuring and cubing butter much easier.

1 tbsp (15 ml) apple cider or white vinegar

¾ cup (177 ml) nondairy milk, soy works best

2 cups (250 g) flour

2 tsp (8 g) sugar

1 tsp salt

1 tbsp (11 g) baking powder

½ cup (115 g) vegan butter, cut in ½-inch (13-mm) cubes and chilled in the freezer for 20 minutes

Preheat the oven to 450°F (232°C). Line a baking sheet with parchment or lightly coat a cast-iron skillet with oil. Either works great.

Add the vinegar to the nondairy milk and set aside for at least 5 minutes. This is your vegan version of buttermilk.

Add the flour, sugar, salt and baking powder to a large bowl. Whisk to combine the ingredients evenly. Take the butter cubes out of the freezer and cut into the flour mixture with a pastry knife or fork until the butter pieces are pea-sized.

Pour ½ cup (120 ml) of the buttermilk over the flour mixture. Toss with a fork to combine, working the dough as little as possible. Pour in another ¼ cup (60 ml) of buttermilk over any flour mixture left dry. Work it in as quickly as possible. The dough will be loose and raggy. Do a few quick, soft kneads to form a ball.

Turn the dough out onto a lightly floured work surface. Roll into a 9 x 12–inch (23 x 30–cm) rectangle, or thereabouts. Cut the rectangle in thirds. Stack the three pieces and roll out into another 9 x 12–inch (23 x 30–cm) rectangle. Use a 2-inch (5-cm) biscuit cutter or a small glass to cut out 9 to 12 biscuits.

Bake on a cookie sheet or cast-iron skillet for about 14 to 16 minutes, or until golden.

GRAVY

4 tbsp (57 g) vegan butter, divided

4 oz (113 g) white mushrooms, diced small

3 tbsp (23 g) flour

3 cups (710 ml) nondairy milk, warmed slightly

Salt and pepper

Fresh thyme or rosemary, optional

While the biscuits are baking, melt 1 tablespoon (15 g) of the butter in a deep sauté pan, over medium heat. Add the chopped mushrooms and cook until the mushrooms release their liquid and just start to brown, about 8 minutes.

Add the remaining 3 tablespoons (43 g) of butter to the pan with the mushrooms. Once it melts, sprinkle the flour over the mushrooms and butter. Stir constantly, using a wooden spoon. Once the flour and butter just barely start to brown, 2 to 3 minutes, add 1 cup (240 ml) of the warmed milk and immediately whisk to incorporate. It should be a smooth paste. Continue to add the milk, about ½ cup (120 ml) at a time until you have the desired consistency, about 8 to 10 minutes.

Season generously with salt and pepper and fresh herbs, if desired. Serve over the biscuits.

TIP: You'll want to warm the milk in the microwave for about a minute before you start. Have a whisk handy for incorporating the milk into the flour and butter (a.k.a., the roux). The warm milk and the whisking will ensure you have a smooth, lump-free gravy.

Butternut Squash and Spinach Quiche

Nut-free
Splurge: none
Serves 6 · 75 minutes to prepare

— • —

If you've ever had traditional quiche, you know it's pretty heavy on the eggs. As in, it's entirely made of eggs. This plant-based version uses tofu as a base, and it's surprisingly close in taste and texture to the real thing. Roasted butternut squash, caramelized onions and spinach fill out the body of this savory breakfast pie, making for a satisfying brunch on a fall or winter morning. If you're not up for making your own pie crust, check the dessert aisle at your grocery store for a pre-made vegan one.

1½ tbsp (22 ml) olive oil, divided

1½ cups (210 g) butternut squash, diced small

1 tsp salt

½ tsp black pepper

½ yellow onion, thinly sliced

½ tbsp (7 ml) balsamic vinegar

2 cups (60 g) baby spinach

1 (16-oz [454-g]) package extra-firm tofu, drained

2 tsp (1 g) dried rosemary

½ tsp dried thyme

Salt and pepper

3 tbsp (45 ml) nondairy milk (as needed)

Flaky Pie Crust (page 189)

Preheat the oven to 375°F (191°C). Add ½ tablespoon (7 ml) of olive oil to the butternut squash and toss to coat. Spread squash on a baking sheet and sprinkle with a pinch of salt and pepper. Roast for 20 minutes, or until the squash is soft and starting to turn golden brown, flipping the pieces halfway through.

Meanwhile, heat the remaining tablespoon (15 ml) of olive oil in a pan over medium heat. Add the onion and cook for about 15 minutes, or until the onion begins to caramelize. Add the balsamic vinegar and continue to caramelize the onions for another minute. Remove the onions from heat and transfer to a large mixing bowl.

Remove the squash from the oven and transfer to the mixing bowl with the caramelized onions. Add the baby spinach and set aside. Break up the tofu with your hands and crumble it into the bowl of a food processor. Add rosemary, thyme, salt and pepper. Pour in the nondairy milk and blend until the mixture is creamy and smooth. Adjust seasonings to taste.

Pour the tofu mixture into the mixing bowl to join the onions, squash and spinach. Stir to thoroughly combine. Spoon the mixture into the pie crust and use a spatula to spread it evenly. Bake for 35 to 40 minutes, or until the top is golden and the center is firm and not mushy. Allow the quiche to cool for at least 10 minutes before slicing and serving.

Tofu Scrambled Eggs

Nut-free
Splurge: none
Serves 2—3 • 15 minutes to prepare

● • ◂

These tofu scrambled eggs aren't trying to be anything they're not. You won't find any fancy spices or veggies in this recipe. Just straight-up scrambled tofu, lightly seasoned to get that satisfying flavor you love. While the key to achieving the right color in this recipe is the turmeric, the flavor comes from the miso paste. There are both vegan and non-vegan varieties, so be sure to check the ingredients before you buy.

1 (15-oz [425-g]) package extra-firm tofu

1 tsp yellow miso paste

¼ cup (60 ml) hot water

½ tsp garlic powder

¼ tsp turmeric

Salt and black pepper

Drain the tofu and firmly press between a few layers of paper towel to remove as much water as possible. In a small mixing bowl, add the miso paste to the hot water and stir to dissolve. Mix in the garlic powder and turmeric. Season with a pinch of salt and black pepper.

Heat a non-stick pan over medium heat. If you're not using a non-stick pan, coat it with cooking spray first. Use your hands to crumble the tofu over the pan, breaking up any big chunks with a spatula. Continue to stir tofu over medium heat for 5 to 7 minutes to cook off any remaining liquid. Next, add half of the miso mixture to the tofu and stir to thoroughly combine. Once the liquid has been absorbed, pour in the second half. Continue to stir the tofu until the miso mixture has been completely soaked up, about 5 minutes.

Remove from heat and season the tofu with additional salt and black pepper to taste. Serve immediately with a side of our Crispy Vegan Bacon (page 116) and a piece of whole wheat or gluten-free toast.

Zucchini Banana Bread Muffins

Nut-free, soy-free
Splurge: Top with sliced almonds or walnut pieces
Makes 12 muffins • 45 minutes to prepare

➤ ● ◄

If you know anyone growing zucchini, you're bound to end up with way too much at some point during the summer. And when that bounty hits, let's tuck some of that vegetable goodness into some cute little muffins the children will adore. Packed with zucchini and bananas, I'm turning a blind eye to the sugar and calling this a parenting win. —Katie

1½ cups (195 g) whole wheat flour

½ tsp salt

½ tsp baking soda

¼ tsp baking powder

1 tsp ground cinnamon

1 medium banana, mashed

¼ cup (48 g) sugar

¼ cup (36 g) light brown sugar

¼ cup (60 ml) vegetable oil

½ cup (120 ml) nondairy milk

1 tsp vanilla extract

1½ cups (170 g) zucchini, shredded

Sliced almonds or walnuts, for serving, optional

Preheat the oven to 350°F (177°C). Grease and flour a muffin tin.

Whisk together the flour, salt, baking soda, baking powder and cinnamon in a large mixing bowl.

In a separate bowl, combine the banana, sugar, light brown sugar, vegetable oil, nondairy milk and vanilla extract. Mix until well blended.

Slowly add the wet ingredients and shredded zucchini to the dry ingredients, mixing together until moistened. Pour the batter into your prepared muffin tin and top with optional nuts. Bake for 35 minutes, or until a toothpick comes out clean. Cool the muffins in the pan for about 10 minutes before transferring to a wire rack.

CHAPTER 7

Bite-Size

If you're not typically a fan of snacking between meals, you definitely will be once you go vegan. After all, one of the perks of following a plant-based diet is being able to eat more (and more often) than your omnivorous friends. And that's never a bad thing. Naturally, we've become experts in the art of snacking on a budget and have lots of recipes to share that'll keep you full until your next meal.

Aside from snacks, we also have some great ideas for appetizers and side dishes to serve at your next shindig. Throwing a Super Bowl party? You can't go wrong with Twice-Baked Potato Bites (page 149). And, once you make our Salted Peanut Butter Popcorn (page 128), you'll never be able to host a movie night without it. When hunger strikes, the next few pages will be your go-to guide for vegan smalls and snacks on the cheap.

Salted Peanut Butter Popcorn

Gluten-free, soy-free
Splurge: Use pure maple syrup
Serves 4 • 10 minutes to prepare

> • •

Your favorite movie night popcorn just got upgraded. Seriously, even the fanciest gourmet blend doesn't stand a chance next to this quick and tasty snack. Be careful not to let the syrup simmer for too long, or your sauce will harden as soon as it cools. We suggest using maple/agave-blend syrup because it's less expensive. But if regular maple syrup is all you have on hand, that will work too.

2 tbsp (30 ml) coconut oil

½ cup (100 g) popcorn kernels

¼ cup (60 ml) maple/agave-blend syrup

1½ tbsp (17 g) creamy peanut butter

⅛ tsp salt, plus more to taste

Add the coconut oil and a few popcorn kernels to a large stockpot over medium heat. Cover. Once the first kernel pops, immediately add the rest of the kernels and re-cover. Gently shake the pot while popcorn kernels are popping, lifting the lid to release steam periodically. Once there is a pause of two to three seconds between pops, remove the pot from heat. Transfer the popped popcorn to a large bowl and set aside.

To a small saucepan, add the maple/agave-blend syrup and bring it to a boil. Cook over medium heat for a few minutes until a thick consistency is reached. Remove the syrup from heat and whisk in the peanut butter and salt, stirring until combined.

Drizzle the popcorn with the peanut butter sauce, tossing and stirring as you go to evenly coat the popcorn. Serve warm, adding more salt to taste.

Whole Wheat Baguette

Nut-free, soy-free
Splurge: none
Makes 1 loaf • 2 hours 15 minutes to prepare

● ● ◄

This is the only baguette recipe you'll ever need! Despite being plant-based, this bread is soft, moist and just the right amount of chewy. Like most freshly baked goods, this baguette is best eaten straight out of the oven. If you want to make garlic bread or bruschetta from your loaf, reduce your oven temperature to 350°F (177°C). Once the bread has cooled completely, slice into ½-inch (13-mm) rounds, brush both sides with olive oil (and sprinkle with minced garlic, if desired) and bake for another fifteen minutes until golden brown, flipping the pieces halfway through.

2 cups (260 g) whole wheat flour

1 tsp sea salt

½ tbsp (5 g) instant yeast

½ tbsp (7 ml) olive oil or vegan butter, melted

1 tbsp (8 g) coconut sugar

⅔ cup (160 ml) warm water

Sift the flour, sea salt and instant yeast into a large mixing bowl. Add the oil or melted vegan butter and stir to combine. Meanwhile, dissolve the coconut sugar in warm water. Once dissolved, mix the sugar water into the dry ingredients. If the dough feels dry, add a tablespoon (15 ml) of water. Transfer the dough to a flat surface and knead by hand for 10 to 15 minutes to activate the gluten.

Form the dough into a ball and place it on a baking sheet lined with parchment paper. Brush with water, cover with plastic wrap and allow the dough to rise in a warm, dark place for an hour. After an hour, move the dough to a cutting board and gently deflate, stretch and flatten. To shape the baguette, fold the top edge of the dough down and the bottom edge of the dough up to meet in the middle, creating a seam that runs the length of the bread. Flip the dough over. Using a sharp knife, cut several slits into the top of the dough. Brush with water once again, cover with plastic wrap and allow the dough to rise in a warm, dark spot for an additional 30 minutes.

Preheat the oven to 425°F (218°C).

After 30 minutes, remove the plastic wrap and brush the bread with olive oil. Place the baking sheet in the oven and bake for 10 minutes. Lower the oven temperature to 375°F (191°C) and bake for an additional 5 to 10 minutes, checking the baguette periodically with a toothpick to check for doneness. Once the bread is done baking, transfer to a cooling rack and allow it to sit for at least 30 minutes before serving.

Simple Lentils

Nut-free, soy-free, gluten-free
Splurge: none
Serves 4 • 35 minutes to prepare

➤ ● ◄

This uncomplicated recipe adds some much-needed flavor to your everyday lentils, making them a welcome addition to salads or our Cauliflower Steaks (page 30). We like to use balsamic vinegar in our lentils, but red wine or rice vinegar would work well too.

1 cup (200 g) brown lentils	Rinse the lentils well and make sure to remove any debris.
3 cups (710 ml) vegetable broth	Bring the vegetable broth to a boil in a small saucepan. Add the lentils and bay leaf. Reduce heat to a simmer and cook for approximately 30 minutes or until the lentils are just soft.
1 bay leaf	
1 tbsp (15 ml) balsamic vinegar	
Salt and pepper	Drain the lentils and remove the bay leaf. Return the lentils to the pot, stir in the vinegar and season with salt and pepper to taste.

Sesame Broccoli

Nut-free, gluten-free
Splurge: none
Serves 4 • 15 minutes to prepare

— ● ◗

We'll be the first to admit that raw broccoli can be pretty unpalatable. But, when it's steamed and drizzled with sesame oil and soy sauce, this polarizing veggie can be downright drool-worthy. If you don't have a steamer basket, you can just as easily cook your broccoli in the microwave. Simply put the florets in a glass dish with about an inch (25 mm) of water, cover with a wet paper towel and heat for two to three minutes. You want the broccoli to be bright green and tender, yet still crunchy.

4 cups (946 ml) water

1 head broccoli, chopped into florets

1 tbsp (15 ml) soy sauce or tamari

½ tbsp (7 ml) sesame oil

1 tsp sesame seeds

⅛ tsp crushed red pepper flakes

In a large pot fitted with a steamer basket, bring water to a simmer over medium-high heat. Add the broccoli florets to the steamer basket and cover. Steam for 4 to 5 minutes, or until tender. Meanwhile, combine the soy sauce or tamari, sesame oil, sesame seeds and crushed red pepper flakes in a small bowl. Mix until well combined. Transfer the broccoli to a serving bowl and drizzle with the sauce. Serve warm.

Pineapple Fried Rice

Nut-free, gluten-free
Splurge: Use fresh pineapple instead of canned
Serves 4 • 20 minutes to prepare

— • —

While traveling through Asia, I ate at a restaurant in Vietnam that served pineapple fried rice straight out of a pineapple. The recipe that follows certainly isn't authentic, but it's sweet, savory and delicious nonetheless. If you're worried about the jalapeño, feel free to omit it. However, once it's sautéed, the spice level is tolerable for nearly every palate. Oh, and if you can find fresh pineapple at a reasonable price, I highly recommend using it as a serving bowl. —Kate

1 tbsp (15 ml) canola oil

½ onion, diced

3 cloves garlic, minced

1 red bell pepper, diced

1½ cups (250 g) canned pineapple, drained and diced

1 jalapeño, seeded and diced

½ cup (25 g) green onion, thinly sliced

2 tbsp (30 ml) soy sauce or tamari

1 tbsp (8 g) coconut sugar

2 cups (322 g) cooked brown rice, cold

½ lime, juiced

Add the canola oil to a large skillet and heat over medium. Stir in the onion and garlic and cook until fragrant, about 3 minutes. Add the red bell pepper, pineapple and jalapeño to the skillet. Turn to medium-high heat. Stir constantly until the liquid has evaporated, about 7 minutes. Sprinkle in the green onion and cook for 30 seconds. Remove from heat.

Combine the soy sauce and coconut sugar in a small bowl and microwave for 20 seconds to dissolve the mixture. Return the skillet to medium heat and add the rice, stirring occasionally to combine it with the other ingredients. Cook until the moisture from the rice has evaporated, about 5 minutes. Add the soy sauce mixture and stir to fully combine. Remove from heat and stir in the lime juice. Allow the fried rice to cool slightly before serving.

Creamiest Pinto Beans

Nut-free, soy-free, gluten-free
Splurge: Use fresh oregano and serve with fresh cilantro and avocado
Serves 6–8 · 90 minutes to prepare + soaking time

➤ ● ◀

Warm and creamy, these pinto beans are perfect over short-grain brown rice with fresh steamed vegetables. They're also the ideal entry to mastering the art of cooking dried beans, a must for any vegan keeping to a budget. And don't be discouraged if your first attempt is unsuccessful. Every batch of dried beans is a little different. You'll get the feel for it after a few tries and make this recipe your own.

2 cups (400 g) pinto beans, rinsed

6 cups (1.4 L) water

2 tsp (1 g) oregano

1 bay leaf

½ yellow onion, quartered

Salt and pepper

Fresh cilantro and avocado, for serving, optional

Soak the beans overnight or at least 6 hours. Drain and rinse.

Add the beans and water to a saucepan. Bring to a boil. Cook at a vigorous boil for about 15 minutes. Skim the foam off the top. Our favorite skimming method is to swirl a ladle gently in the middle of the pot. All of the foam will naturally gravitate to the sides of the pot where you can easily capture it.

Add the oregano, bay leaf and onion, and continue to cook at a gentle simmer for about another 90 minutes, or until the beans are very soft. If your dried beans are old, it's going to take considerably longer for them to cook through. Check the beans about every 20 to 30 minutes to make sure they're still covered in water; if not, add another cup or two (240 to 480 ml) until the beans are just covered.

You'll know they're ready when they start to look creamy and stick to the bottom of the pan. When that happens, turn off the heat, give them a few really hearty stirs to break up the beans and scrape everything off the bottom of the pan. Put the lid back on and let them sit for another 10 minutes to thicken up if they're too thin.

Remove the onion and bay leaf. Generously add salt and pepper to taste. Smash some of the beans against the side of the pot until you've reached the desired creaminess. Serve with optional fresh cilantro and avocado, if desired.

Orange Glazed Tofu

Nut-free, gluten-free
Splurge: none
Serves 4 • 1 hour 45 minutes to prepare

• ▪ ◂

Nearly everyone can remember getting Chinese food and ordering orange chicken. Its fluorescent, unnatural, gooey appearance almost made it look extraterrestrial, didn't it? The recipe below calls on some of the same flavors from your favorite Chinese dish, but you won't need sunglasses to eat it. Not to mention, this version is totally plant-based and free of yucky additives!

1 (14-oz [400-g]) package extra-firm tofu

¼ cup (60 ml) soy sauce or tamari

2 tbsp (30 ml) rice vinegar

1 tbsp (15 ml) olive oil

½ tsp red pepper flakes

⅛ tsp garlic powder

ORANGE GLAZE

¼ cup and 2 tbsp (90 ml) orange juice

½ tsp agave

¼ tsp ginger

1 tsp cornstarch

1 tsp water

Drain the tofu and press between a few layers of paper towel to remove as much liquid as possible. Then slice the tofu into ½-inch (13-mm) slabs and press with paper towels again. To make the marinade, whisk together the soy sauce, rice vinegar, olive oil, red pepper flakes and garlic powder in a small mixing bowl. Set aside.

Arrange the tofu slices in a single layer in a shallow baking dish. Pour the marinade over the tofu, flipping the pieces and moving them around until each is thoroughly covered. Put the tofu in the refrigerator for at least 1 hour, flipping the tofu halfway through to absorb all of the marinade.

Preheat the oven to 400°F (204°C). Bake the tofu for 30 minutes, flipping each piece halfway through. Meanwhile, make your orange glaze by combining the orange juice, agave and ginger in a small saucepan. Heat over medium-low until the mixture reaches a gentle simmer. In a small mixing bowl, dissolve the cornstarch in the water. Then pour the dissolved cornstarch into the saucepan to join the orange juice mixture. Continue to stir over medium-low heat until the glaze thickens, 3 to 5 minutes. Remove from heat and set aside.

Take the tofu out of the oven and brush each side with the orange glaze. Return the tofu to the oven and cook until the glaze begins to caramelize, about 5 minutes. Serve immediately with a side of Sesame Broccoli (page 133) or in our Rainbow Sushi Rolls (page 23). It also refrigerates well, if you want to use it as extra protein in your favorite salads throughout the week.

Baked Oven Fries with Rosemary and Sea Salt

Nut-free, soy-free, gluten-free
Splurge: Pair with our Cucumber Tzatziki Sauce (page 164) for dipping
Serves 4 • 50 minutes to prepare

━ • ━

My kids have a thing for those chicken-less nuggets. I'm sure this is nothing new to any parent out there, but they're obsessed. And occasionally I buckle to their tiny demands. Needless to say they are far from my favorite, so pairing them with these wonderfully fragrant rosemary fries and a nice salad gives me something to look forward to on nugget night. —Katie

4 medium potatoes, any variety works great

1½ tbsp (20 ml) olive oil

2–3 sprigs rosemary

Salt and pepper

Cucumber Tzatziki Sauce (page 164), for serving, optional

Preheat the oven to 400°F (204°C). Line a baking sheet with parchment paper. Set aside.

Scrub and rinse the potatoes well. Cut into wedges. Mine usually end up a mix of wedges and thick fries. Uniformity of thickness is the important part.

Toss the potatoes, olive oil, rosemary and salt and pepper in a large bowl. Pour out onto the baking sheet. If the fries are too crowded, use a second baking sheet. Overcrowding causes them to steam instead of crisp up, and no one likes that.

Bake for about 40 minutes or until desired crispness, turning about halfway through. Serve with optional Cucumber Tzatziki Sauce, if desired.

Sun-Dried Tomato White Bean Hummus

Nut-free, soy-free
Splurge: none
Serves 4–6 • 5 minutes to prepare

• • •

If you've ever made or eaten traditional hummus, you know it's made from a blend of chickpeas and tahini. But we like to break the rules, so we made it with white beans. The result is an ultra-creamy spread that offers a nice change of flavor from the stuff you're used to. If you can find them, we recommend buying your sun-dried tomatoes in a package, rather than a jar. They're way less messy and typically more affordable than the varieties swimming in olive oil. If you do buy sun-dried tomatoes in a jar, be sure to drain them thoroughly before chopping.

1 (15-oz [425-g]) can white beans, drained and rinsed

½ lemon, juiced

2 garlic cloves, minced

¼ cup (38 g) sun-dried tomatoes, chopped

¼ cup (60 ml) olive oil

¼ tsp salt

⅛ tsp pepper

Combine the white beans, lemon juice, garlic, sun-dried tomatoes, olive oil, salt and pepper in a food processor. Blend until the hummus is completely smooth. Adjust seasonings to taste. Transfer the hummus to an airtight container and chill in the refrigerator until ready to eat. Serve with sliced veggies, pita chips or slathered on your favorite bagel.

Roasted Baby Bok Choy

Nut-free, gluten-free
Splurge: none
Serves 2–4 • 20 minutes to prepare

◗ ● ◖

This bok choy is guaranteed to kick up your ramen game with all of its savory roasted goodness. It's a shame if you can't find the baby variety, but full size works just as well. Just know it will be ever-so-slightly less cute.

3–4 heads baby bok choy, quartered lengthwise

1½ tbsp (22 ml) olive oil

¼ tsp red pepper flakes

2 tsp (10 ml) soy sauce or tamari

1 clove garlic, minced

Preheat the oven to 450°F (232°C). Line a baking sheet with parchment paper.

Lay out the bok choy on the baking sheet, spaced evenly.

Mix all the remaining ingredients in a small bowl. Drizzle half the oil mixture over bok choy, turn and drizzle over the other side.

Bake for 10 minutes, turn, and bake another 5 minutes or until the ends just start to get crispy.

Pineapple Slaw

Nut-free, soy-free, gluten-free
Splurge: none
Serves 4 • 10 minutes to prepare

— • • —

As a soggy side item that barely gets touched at barbecues, coleslaw has a bad rap—with good reason. Traditional coleslaw consists of finely shredded cabbage drenched in mayonnaise. For those who despise both of those things, coleslaw is the grim reaper of picnic foods. This recipe is the opposite of all of these things. While coleslaw wouldn't be coleslaw without cabbage, we use a sweet and sour dressing of avocado and pineapple to give this scorned side dish a much-needed makeover.

½ ripe avocado, mashed

⅓ cup (55 g) crushed pineapple, drained

2 tbsp (5 g) cilantro leaves, torn

½ tbsp (7 ml) agave

1 lime, juiced

½ tsp apple cider vinegar

2 cups (680 g) purple cabbage, shredded

Salt and pepper, to taste

Combine the mashed avocado, pineapple, cilantro, agave, lime juice and apple cider vinegar in a mixing bowl. Whisk to combine, adding a bit of water to thin as necessary. Once you have a nice creamy dressing, stir in the cabbage, toss to thoroughly combine and season with salt and pepper to taste. Serve immediately with our BBQ Chickpea Sliders (page 19) or atop your favorite vegan burger.

Spicy Chipotle Corn and Zucchini

Nut-free, soy-free, gluten-free
Splurge: Top with fresh cilantro
Serves 4 • 10 minutes to prepare

➤ ● ◄

If you don't already have chipotle pepper on hand, it is a must for adding to your pantry staples. It's inexpensive and an incredibly flavorful and versatile spice you can use to add a smoky heat to almost anything.

½ tbsp (7 ml) olive oil

1 clove garlic, mashed

1 medium zucchini

1½ cups (217 g) frozen corn

¼ tsp chipotle

¼ tsp salt

Fresh cilantro, for serving, optional

Heat the olive oil in a large sauté pan over medium heat. Add garlic and cook for just a minute. Add the zucchini and cook for about 3 minutes, until it just starts to brown but isn't yet soft.

Add the corn, chipotle and salt. Toss to coat evenly and cook until the corn is warmed through and the zucchini is just done, 3 to 4 minutes. Top with optional fresh cilantro, if desired.

Cilantro Lime Rice

Nut-free, soy-free, gluten-free
Splurge: none
Serves 4–6 • 45 minutes to prepare

▶ ● ◀

I'll be the first to admit that it took me YEARS to learn how to make rice. Yes, rice. What should be the most insanely easy thing to cook I was miserable at. Sticky, check. Burnt, check. Hard, check. I made every misstep in the book. I tried stove-top methods, rice cookers, rinsing, not rinsing, jasmine, short grain, basmati. Ugh. I was exhausted and tired of eating lame rice. I wanted to make rice like you get at the little Thai place down the street. Is that too much to expect? I didn't think so; I dug in. The truth is, you need to disregard everything you've ever read on a bag of rice. Now we can begin.

The tried and not-so-true 2:1 ratio is hooey. For long grain go with 1¼ cups (295 ml) water per 1 cup (210 g) of rice. For short grain, try 1½ cups (355 ml) water per 1 cup (210 g) of rice. —Katie

3 cups (710 ml) water

1 tsp salt, divided

2 cups (421 g) short-grain brown rice

½ cup (20 g) fresh cilantro, chopped

1 lime, zested and juiced

A shallow pot with a tight-fitting lid works best for cooking rice. Add the water, rice and ½ teaspoon salt to the pot. Bring to a boil over medium-high heat. Once it's boiling, turn the heat down to low or medium-low so the rice continues to cook at a very soft boil. Remove from the heat after 30 minutes and let the pot sit covered (no peeking) for another 10.

Mix in the cilantro, lime juice and remaining salt.

Twice-Baked Potato Bites

Nut-free, soy-free, gluten-free
Splurge: Use fresh chives in place of dried
Serves 4–6 • 60 minutes to prepare

━ ● ◄

Bust out the melon baller. You've got tiny potatoes to scoop out and that's the perfect tool for the job. If you don't have a baller, any small spoon will work. When it comes time for scooping, be sure to wait until the potatoes are cool before you scoop. Those little spuds can really hold their heat.

2 lb (907 g) red new potatoes (about 14), halved

1 tbsp (15 ml) olive oil

Coarse salt and ground pepper

¾ cup (90 g) Vegan Sour Cream (page 167)

2 tbsp (6 g) chives, plus more for garnish

Preheat the oven to 450°F (232°C). Line a rimmed baking sheet with parchment paper.

Cut a thin slice off the bottom of each of your halved potatoes, so they sit flat. In a large bowl, toss the potatoes with oil; season with salt and pepper and arrange bottom-side down on the baking sheet. Bake until tender, 30 to 35 minutes. Let them cool on the sheet.

When the potatoes are cool enough, scoop out about a teaspoon from the center of each potato and place in a medium bowl. Add vegan sour cream and chives, and mash; season with salt and pepper. Stuff the potatoes with the filling.

Bake the potatoes until lightly browned, about 15 minutes.

CHAPTER 8

Get Sauced

Sauces can transform any dish from mediocre to magnificent with nothing more than a drizzle, dab or dollop. You'll find the following sauces referenced in different recipes throughout this book, but don't be afraid to mix and match. You want to boost your Burrito Bowl (page 54) with Miso Garlic Dressing (page 155) instead of Cilantro Tahini (page 152)? Go for it! These sauces are designed to be not only budget-friendly, but versatile enough to become your go-to guide for adding a pop of flavor to any dish in your repertoire.

On the pages ahead, you'll find all the sauces you need to take the flavor of your salads, bowls, pastas and mains to the next level. Even your soups and chilis can be transformed when topped with our Vegan Sour Cream (page 167), which tastes even better than the real thing. When you find a sauce you like, don't hesitate to double or triple the recipe and keep it in a mason jar in the fridge. That way, you always have a delicious sauce on hand to add some last-minute flavor to whatever's on your dinner table.

Cilantro Tahini

Nut-free, soy-free, gluten-free
Splurge: none
Serves 4–6 • 5 minutes to prepare

- ● ◄

Tahini is made from ground sesame seeds and is a really popular condiment in Middle Eastern cuisine. As vegans, we love it for its smooth, creamy appeal and use it anywhere we darn-well please. In this recipe, you'll combine it with cilantro and lime juice to create a lovely, tart sauce you can use to dress your favorite salads or bowls. Heck, you can even drizzle it on roasted veggies or use it as a dipping sauce for toasted pita bread.

⅓ cup (60 g) tahini
¼ cup and 1 tbsp (75 ml) water
1 cup (40 g) fresh cilantro leaves
1 tbsp (15 ml) lime juice
½ tsp salt

Combine the tahini, water, cilantro, lime juice and salt in a blender or food processor. Blend until smooth. Serve with our Burrito Bowl (page 54).

Miso Garlic Dressing

Nut-free
Splurge: none
Serves 4–6 • 10 minutes to prepare

— • —

Miso is more than a fermented nutritional powerhouse. It brings its distinctive salty tang to this easy-to-make dressing. Versatile enough to add to noodles, vegetables or rice. We usually whip this up in a mini food processor, but a whisk would work just fine. If you are whisking, mince the garlic well before you get started.

1 tbsp (15 g) white miso paste

2–3 cloves garlic

2 tbsp (30 ml) lemon juice

2 tbsp (30 ml) seasoned rice vinegar

1 tbsp (15 ml) water

¼ cup (60 ml) extra virgin olive oil

Add the miso paste, garlic, lemon juice, rice vinegar and water to the (small) bowl of a food processor. With the processor running, add the olive oil in a thin stream through the spout. Blend until well combined.

TIP: If you don't have seasoned rice vinegar, you can use regular rice vinegar and add a little maple syrup or agave.

Thai Peanut Sauce

Gluten-free
Splurge: none
Serves 4 · 5 minutes to prepare

— • ◂

Peanut butter and soy sauce and ginger—oh my! This sauce is an absolute flavor explosion on anything from steamed veggies to noodles. The great thing about fresh ginger is that it's easy to buy only what you need. You don't need to take home the entire root! Just break off a tiny chunk and you'll save a ton at the checkout line. You can also use ¼ teaspoon ground ginger, if you must. But fresh ginger really adds a lot to this Asian-inspired sauce.

¼ cup (45 g) smooth peanut butter

3 tbsp (45 ml) soy sauce or tamari

1 tsp fresh ginger, grated

1 tbsp (15 ml) agave

1 tbsp (15 ml) rice vinegar

1 tsp sesame oil

½ lime, juiced

Pinch of red pepper flakes

Mix the peanut butter and soy sauce in a microwave-safe bowl and heat until the peanut butter is soft and easy to stir, about 30 seconds. Add the ginger, agave, rice vinegar, sesame oil, lime juice and red pepper flakes. Whisk together to fully incorporate the flavors, adding water to thin as necessary. Serve with our Crunchy Thai Salad (page77) or Thai Peanut Noodles (page 49).

Simple Vinaigrette

Nut-free, soy-free, gluten-free
Splurge: none
Serves 4 • 5 minutes to prepare

— • ◂

Often, salad dressings are so loaded with pungent ingredients (and gross additives) that they completely mask the flavor of the dish. When you make a salad and want the fruits or veggies to do the talking, go with this simple vinaigrette. It's light enough to allow the beautiful flavors of your salad to shine through, with just a touch of sweetness to balance the acidity. Truly, you can't go wrong with this one.

¼ cup (60 ml) white wine vinegar

1½ tsp (7 ml) olive oil

1 tbsp (15 ml) agave

Salt and pepper, to taste

Add all of the ingredients to a small bowl and whisk thoroughly to combine. Serve with our Kale Salad with Cherries and Almonds (page 86) or any salad that needs a light and simple dressing.

Sriracha Mayo

Nut-free, gluten-free
Splurge: none
Serves 4 • 5 minutes to prepare

- ● ◂

There are people who love mayonnaise, and there are those who hate it. If you belong to the former category, you're going to like this recipe. While it would be impossible to achieve the exact taste of your favorite store-bought brand, our plant-based version has the silky consistency and acidic flavor that make it work wonderfully as a spread. If you're averse to Sriracha, feel free to swap it for your favorite hot sauce. Or leave it out completely. It's your sandwich.

1 cup (248 g) soft tofu

2 tbsp (30 ml) olive oil

2 tbsp (30 ml) apple cider vinegar

2 tsp (10 ml) Dijon mustard

1½ tsp (7 ml) Sriracha sauce

½ tsp agave

¼ tsp salt

Press the tofu between paper towels to remove as much water as possible. Then add all of the ingredients to a food processor and blend until very smooth. Adjust the seasonings to taste and serve as a spread on our BLT with Sriracha Mayo (page 22).

Chimichurri Sauce

Nut-free, soy-free, gluten-free
Splurge: none
Serves 2 • 5 minutes to prepare

◗ ● ◖

Chimichurri gets its distinct flavor from fresh herbs. No substituting for dry spices here! To cut down on your grocery bill, consider planting an herb garden on your kitchen windowsill. Cilantro can be finicky, but parsley doesn't require much light or maintenance once it gets going. This simple sauce adds an explosion of flavor to everything from grilled veggies to black bean burgers. Try it once, and you'll want to eat it on everything!

¼ cup (60 ml) apple cider vinegar

2 garlic cloves, minced

½ jalapeño, chopped

½ tsp sea salt

¼ cup (10 g) fresh parsley, chopped

½ cup (20 g) fresh cilantro, chopped

¼ cup (60 ml) extra-virgin olive oil

Combine the apple cider vinegar, garlic, jalapeño and sea salt in a medium bowl. Stir in the parsley and cilantro, and then whisk in the olive oil. Refrigerate until ready to serve with our Sweet Potato Steaks with Chimichurri Sauce (page 20) or atop your favorite vegan burger.

Orange Chia Dressing

Nut-free, soy-free
Splurge: none
Serves 4 • 5 minutes to prepare

◗ ● ◖

Salad dressings are notorious for being filled with icky ingredients, lots of sugar and even more salt. With all of the additives you're pouring on your veggies, what's the point of eating a salad at all? This homemade dressing tastes just as good as what you can buy in a bottle, and it's a billion times healthier. Fresh orange juice and chia seeds play the leading roles, providing an extra boost of nutrients to your bowl of greens.

¼ cup (60 ml) olive oil

3 tbsp (45 ml) orange juice

½ tsp orange zest

2 tsp (6 g) chia seeds

½ tsp agave

¼ tsp white wine vinegar

⅛ tsp salt

Combine all of the ingredients in a mixing bowl and whisk until blended. Serve immediately with our Grilled Romaine and Beet Salad (page 74) or store in an airtight container in the refrigerator for up to a week.

Curry Dressing

Nut-free, gluten-free
Splurge: none
Serves 4 • 5 minutes to prepare

— • —

Holy smokes, does this sauce pack a lot of flavor! This might be the only time in this book we recommend not buying the bargain brand. The quality of the curry powder you buy will have a huge impact on how this sauce tastes. That said, you don't have to visit a boutique spice shop to get a fancy blend. McCormick makes a fantastic one you can find in pretty much every grocery store, and it won't break the bank.

⅔ cup (165 g) soft tofu

2 tsp (10 ml) apple cider vinegar

1 tbsp (7 g) curry powder

½ tbsp (7 ml) Dijon mustard

¼ tsp sea salt

¼ tsp black pepper

Combine the soft tofu, apple cider vinegar, curry powder, Dijon mustard, salt and pepper in a food processor. Blend until you've achieved a smooth consistency and all of the ingredients are fully mixed, scraping down the sides of the bowl as needed. Transfer the dressing to a bowl and season with additional salt and pepper to taste. Serve immediately with our Curried Potato Salad (page 75) or store in an airtight container in the refrigerator and use it as a sandwich spread.

Cucumber Tzatziki Sauce

Nut-free, gluten-free
Splurge: Use fresh dill and parsley instead of dried
Serves 4 • 5 minutes to prepare

— • —

Tzatziki sauce is popular in Greek cuisine and is often served as a condiment on gyro sandwiches. Though traditional Tzatziki is made with strained yogurt, we think you'll find the taste and texture of this plant-based version to be spot on. You can use it to add a garlicky zip to any Mediterranean-inspired dish, as a sandwich spread or to replace sour cream on a baked potato. Really, there is no wrong answer! This stuff is good on everything.

1 cup (248 g) soft tofu

½ lemon, juiced

½ cup (60 g) cucumber, diced

1 tsp dried dill

1 tsp dried parsley

1 small garlic clove, minced

¼ tsp salt

⅛ tsp black pepper

Press the tofu with paper towels to remove as much water as possible. Combine all of the ingredients in a blender or food processor and blend until silky smooth. Serve with our Falafel Bowl with Israeli Couscous (page 58) or our Mediterranean Stuffed Peppers (page 29).

Mushroom Gravy

Nut-free, soy-free
Splurge: Use crimini or portobello mushrooms
Serves 4–6 • 20 minutes to prepare

— • • ◀

Gravies are often left to the last minute, in a mad gravy dash, as everything else hits the table. But there's really no need; you can make just about any gravy ahead of time and it reheats perfectly.

3 cups (710 ml) vegetable broth

3 tbsp (43 g) vegan butter, divided

8 oz (227 g) white button mushrooms, chopped into small pieces

2 tbsp (15 g) flour

Salt and pepper, to taste

Warm your broth in a small saucepan.

Heat a skillet over medium-high heat and melt 1 tablespoon (14 g) of vegan butter. Add the mushrooms and cook until the liquid is released and they begin to soften, 8 to 10 minutes. Add the remaining butter to the pan and let it melt. Sprinkle the pan with the flour, stirring constantly until the flour just starts to brown, about 3 minutes.

Slowly add the vegetable broth, ½ cup (120 ml) at a time while whisking. Let the gravy thicken slightly between additions of broth. Simmer until thickened to desired consistency, about 10 minutes, adding more broth if needed. Add salt and pepper to taste.

TIP: The secret to smooth, lump-free gravy is the first addition of broth to the flour and butter mixture (aka, the roux). You'll want to start by warming up your broth. Then add between ¼ and ½ cup (60 and 120 ml) to the roux, whisking constantly until smooth.

Vegan Sour Cream

Nut-free, soy-free, gluten-free
Splurge: none
Makes ½ cup (60 g) · 15 minutes to prepare

► ● ◄

Sour cream is one of those condiments you don't realize you love until you eat your favorite dish without it. Like chili, for example. What good is a bowl of hot, vegan chili without a cool dab of sour cream on top? Enchiladas are another example. Sour cream adds an entirely new layer of texture and flavor you can't get with any other topping. Our Vegan Sour Cream uses nothing more than coconut milk, lemon (or lime) juice and salt to send your spiciest dishes into creamy-cool oblivion.

1 (15-oz [425-g]) can full-fat coconut milk, chilled in the refrigerator overnight

3 tsp (15 ml) lemon or lime juice

⅛ tsp salt

Put the can of coconut milk in the fridge overnight to allow the cream to separate from the water. Once the can is completely chilled, flip it over and open from the bottom. Pour the coconut water into an airtight container and pop it in the refrigerator. You can save it for the next time you make a smoothie. Carefully scoop the coconut cream into a mixing bowl, and add the lemon or lime juice and salt. Whisk the ingredients together to combine the flavors and eliminate any lumps. Continue to stir until the mixture is smooth and creamy. Serve atop our Black Bean and Tempeh Chili (page 99) or in our Mushroom Stroganoff (page 40).

Sesame Salad Dressing

Nut-free, gluten-free
Splurge: none
Makes about ½ cup (120 ml) • 5 minutes to prepare

● ● ◄

This versatile salad dressing is so simple but so effective at adding flavor to your favorite veggie-forward, Asian-inspired meals. Think tofu bowls, pot stickers, ramen noodles, salads and even sushi rolls. If you have enough ingredients on hand, don't hesitate to double the recipe and store a batch of this dressing in your fridge for easy access. If you eat Thai and Japanese food as much as we do, this stuff will disappear in a flash.

⅓ cup (78 ml) soy sauce or tamari

2 tbsp (24 g) coconut sugar (or brown sugar)

2 tsp (10 ml) sesame oil

½ tsp red chili pepper flakes

1 tbsp (15 ml) water

Mix all of the ingredients together in a small, microwave-safe bowl. Microwave in 15-second intervals, stirring after each round, until the sugar dissolves into the liquid. Serve immediately with our Chilled Soba Noodle Salad (page 82) or store in an airtight container in the fridge.

Chunky Marinara Sauce

Nut-free, soy-free, gluten-free
Splurge: none
Serves 10–12 • 30 minutes to prepare

— • —

Pasta with marinara sauce is one of the cheapest, easiest plant-based meals you can make. It can also taste quite gourmet if you invest a little time in making your own sauce. This recipe comes together in under 30 minutes, and most of it is hands off. Bonus: You probably have a lot of the ingredients in your pantry already. If your garden happens to be extremely productive this season, you can swap the canned tomatoes for 20 to 25 fresh, peeled tomatoes.

1 tbsp (15 ml) olive oil

½ onion, diced

4 cloves garlic, minced

2 (28-oz [794-g]) cans crushed tomatoes

1 tsp dried basil

1½ tsp (1 g) dried oregano

3 tsp (12 g) sugar

1 tsp salt

¼ tsp crushed red pepper, optional

In a large saucepan, heat the olive oil over medium heat. Add the onion and garlic and cook until soft, about 5 minutes. Pour in the crushed tomatoes and season with basil, oregano, sugar, salt and crushed red pepper. Stir well and reduce to medium-low heat. Simmer for 25 to 30 minutes to allow the flavors to blend together, stirring periodically. Serve immediately with our Spaghetti with Lentil "Meatballs" (page 43) or Kale Stuffed Shells with Marinara (page 39) or freeze in an airtight container for up to a month.

See image on page 150.

CHAPTER 9

Glazed and Infused

From our experiences across potlucks, office parties and barbecues, there are three camps when it comes to desserts: the healthy camp, the chocolate camp and the anything-sweet camp. We admire those who are firmly in the healthy camp. They take full advantage of the best produce the seasons have to offer, which is ideal when adhering to a budget. On the other hand, chocolate lovers have the advantage of whipping up something amazing with nothing more than a few pantry staples.

Most of the time, you'll find us firmly planted in the anything-sweet camp. We swoon at the sight of melty chocolate chips in freshly baked cookies, a thin glaze running down the side of a warm cake and a perfectly grilled peach. Regardless of which camp you're in, you'll absolutely find something to make, share and enjoy in our roundup of the best budget vegan desserts.

Frozen Chocolate Banana Swirl

Nut-free, soy-free, gluten-free
Splurge: none
Serves 4 • 15 minutes to prepare

— • ◄

When summer delivers ice cream weather, by all means we abide with enthusiasm and a brilliant three-ingredient recipe: the chocolate banana swirl. Just cut up the bananas, freeze and swirl with your favorite flavors. We have some real chocoholics under our roof, but you could use anything—frozen strawberries, blueberries or a little vanilla extract.

4 bananas, cut into 1-inch (25-mm)
pieces and frozen

2 tbsp (14 g) unsweetened cocoa
powder

Nondairy milk, just a splash to get things
moving in your blender

OPTIONAL MIX-INS, FROM MOST TO
LEAST HEALTHY

Hemp seeds

Vegan protein powder

Almond butter or other nut butter

Blueberries

Strawberries

Vanilla

Vegan chocolate chips

Oreos

OPTIONAL TOPPINGS

Chopped nuts

Fresh fruit

Roasted coconut chips

Drop all of your ingredients into the blender and blend until creamy. Serve immediately with desired toppings. The natural consistency of this dessert is like soft-serve ice cream. If you want something more scoop-able, put it in the freezer for up to an hour. Careful, though. If you leave it in any longer than an hour you'll have a giant popsicle, and not in a good way.

Coconut Peach Popsicles

Nut-free, soy-free, gluten-free
Splurge: Add a few sprigs fresh basil or mint to the blender
Makes 4 • 10 minutes plus time to freeze

━ ● ◄

Come summer, our house overfloweth with peaches. Ripe summer fruit is a temptation I cannot overcome, especially when it's on sale. Then my big pile of peaches are in their prime en masse and I'm in a mad dash to make everything peachy. This recipe came from just such a fit. It's simple enough for kids to help with and the perfect dessert for warm summer nights. —Katie

1 ripe peach

1 (6-oz [170-g]) container vanilla coconut milk yogurt

¼ cup (60 ml) water

Fresh basil or mint, optional

Cut the peach into quarters, discarding the pit. Place all of the ingredients into a blender. Blend until smooth and pour into popsicle molds to freeze. Freeze for 3 to 4 hours before serving.

Watermelon Lime Granitas

Nut-free, soy-free, gluten-free
Splurge: none
Serves 4–6 • 20 minutes plus freeze time

● ● ◄

What this recipe demands in passive time, it makes up for in simplicity. We find a 9 x 13–inch (23 x 33–cm) pan works best for this—it gives you a little slosh room getting into the freezer. With a steady hand, a smaller pan would work just fine. If you want to make this a grownup dessert, vodka or tequila is a superb addition.

¼ cup (48 g) sugar

3 tbsp (45 ml) water

2 limes, juice and zest

1 small watermelon

Warm the sugar, water and lime juice in a saucepan at a gentle simmer until the sugar is completely dissolved and the mixture starts to thicken just slightly, about 10 minutes. Remove from heat and let the syrup cool.

While the syrup is cooling, cut your watermelon into chunks, discarding the rind and any seeds.

Blend the watermelon chunks in a blender until smooth. You should have about 3 cups (455 g). Add the cooled syrup and lime zest to the watermelon.

Transfer to a 9 x 13–inch (23 x 33–cm) baking dish. Place the dish ever so carefully in the freezer. If you can't fit a 9 x 13–inch (23 x 33–cm) dish in your freezer, a loaf pan or a 9 x 9–inch (23 x 23–cm) dish will work as well.

Check in on your granitas every half hour or so. Give it a quick scrape over with a fork so it doesn't freeze solid and develops a nice, fluffy texture.

Mini Key Lime Pies

Nut-free
Splurge: none
Serves 12 • 35 minutes to prepare

• • ◄

These mini key lime pies strike a sinfully delicious balance between sweet and tart, and the creamy consistency will have you convinced you're indulging in the real thing. It's like a tropical vacation in your mouth! Of course, no dessert is complete without a crumbly base. While we think our easy, three-ingredient Graham Cracker Pie Crust (page 191) is the perfect complement, you can use pretty much any crust you'd like and these little guys will still taste like a dream.

Graham Cracker Pie Crust (page 191)

12 oz (340 g) firm silken tofu, drained

½ cup (123 g) coconut cream (the solid stuff at the top of a can of coconut milk)

1 tsp vanilla extract

1½ tbsp (14 g) cornstarch

2½ tbsp (40 ml) agave nectar

2½ limes, zested and juiced

Preheat the oven to 350°F (177°C). Make your graham cracker pie crust in muffin tins and set it aside to cool.

Add the tofu, coconut cream, vanilla extract, cornstarch, agave nectar, lime juice and 1 teaspoon of lime zest to a blender and purée until silky smooth, adding a touch more coconut cream as needed. Evenly distribute the key lime pie filling between each of the muffin tin slots, about 2 to 3 tablespoons (31 to 46 g) each. Bake for 15 to 20 minutes, or until pies are firm but jiggly. Lightly sprinkle the remaining lime zest over the key lime pies. Set aside to cool.

Once the key lime pies are cool, put them in the refrigerator and let them chill for 4 to 6 hours, or overnight. They're best eaten within a couple of days, but if you want to store them, they'll stay good in the freezer for one to two weeks.

Walnut Brownie Cookies

Soy-free

Splurge: Add vegan chocolate chips with the walnuts

Makes 12 cookies • 30 minutes to prepare plus 2 hours to chill dough

• • ◄

If you're ever at a loss for what to make—chocolate is the answer. These rich, indulgent little treats are so simple to pull together they're sure to become a regular in your cookie jar. If you don't already have walnuts in your pantry, try looking for them in the bulk bins at your local health food store or the tiny bags in the baking section. Buying just a ½ cup (58 g) will be very budget friendly.

½ cup (120 ml) canola oil

¼ cup (60 ml) nondairy milk

1 cup (192 g) sugar

1 tsp vanilla

¾ cup (94 g) flour

¾ cup (83 g) cocoa powder

½ tsp salt

¼ tsp baking soda

½ cup (58 g) walnuts, chopped

Vegan chocolate chips, optional

Whisk together the canola oil, nondairy milk, sugar and vanilla, and set aside.

In another bowl, combine the flour, cocoa powder, salt and baking soda. Whisk the dry ingredients to combine them evenly. Then, add the wet ingredients and stir (we like to use a wooden spoon) until it comes together in a brownie-like batter. Mix in the walnuts and optional vegan chocolate chips.

Chill the dough for 2 hours or longer.

Preheat the oven to 350°F (177°C). Line two baking sheets with parchment paper. Scoop out rounded tablespoons (15 g) of dough onto the baking sheets. Bake for about 10 to 12 minutes. Remove from the oven and allow the cookies to cool completely before transferring them.

Peanut Butter Oatmeal Bars

Soy-free
Splurge: Mix in ½ cup (80 g) chopped peanuts with the chocolate chips
Makes 12 bars · 60 minutes to prepare, plus time to cool

— ● —

This is a very forgiving recipe, perfect for making with kids. Better yet, it welcomes almost any extra mix-in, so you can really make it your own. We've even been known to fancy it up with a swirl of jam before baking by adding a few generous dollops to the top and swirling with a butter knife. The hardest part about this recipe is waiting for it to cool.

½ cup (96 g) sugar

½ cup (72 g) brown sugar

¼ cup (60 ml) canola oil

½ mashed banana (¼ cup [57 g])

½ cup (90 g) peanut butter

2 tsp (10 ml) pure vanilla extract

½ cup (120 ml) nondairy milk

1 cup (130 g) whole wheat flour

1 cup (80 g) rolled oats

1½ tsp (6 g) baking powder

¼ tsp salt

½ cup (90 g) vegan chocolate chips

Chopped peanuts, optional

Preheat the oven to 350°F (177°C).

Combine the sugar, brown sugar, canola oil, banana, peanut butter, vanilla and nondairy milk in a bowl and whisk until smooth.

In a separate bowl, combine the flour, oats, baking powder and salt.

Add the dry ingredients to the wet and stir until just combined. Stir in the chocolate chips and chopped peanuts, if using. Spread into a lightly greased 9 x 9–inch (23 x 23–cm) pan and bake 45 minutes or until the edges are just browned and the center is raised. Let cool for at least an hour before cutting into bars.

Wacky Cake

Nut-free, soy-free
Splurge: Add vegan chocolate chips to the batter and sprinkle with powdered sugar before serving
Serves 8 • 40 minutes to prepare

▬ ● ◄

The Wacky Cake is something just about every grandma and church lady in the midwestern United States can whip up in nothing flat. Maybe you recognize it by another name: the Three-Hole Cake or the Depression Cake. At a time when butter and eggs were scarce or far too expensive, these ingenious women (and maybe even a few men) found a way to make their cakes rise. The solution was simple: baking soda and vinegar—an explosive combination, handy for third grade volcanic science projects and bringing a beautiful rise to a cake batter, sans eggs. It very well may be the original vegan cake. This decades-old recipe is simple, light, spongy and not too sweet. Although, truth be told, I'm always up for adding a few handfuls of chocolate chips to the mix. Never hurts. Oh, and dust with a little powdered sugar just before serving. Channel your inner grandma and bake yourself a wacky cake.

1½ cups (187 g) bleached all-purpose flour

¼ cup (28 g) unsweetened cocoa powder

½ tsp baking soda

½ tsp salt

1 cup (192 g) sugar or evaporated cane juice

1 tsp vanilla extract

1 tbsp (15 ml) white or cider vinegar

6 tbsp (90 ml) vegetable oil

1 cup (240 ml) water

Vegan chocolate chips, optional

Powdered sugar, for serving, optional

Position a rack in the center of the oven and preheat to 375°F (191°C).

Lightly grease an 8- or 9-inch (20- or 23-cm) square pan. In a large mixing bowl, mix the flour, cocoa, baking soda, salt and sugar. Make three holes in the dry ingredients, one large and two small. Add the vanilla to the first small hole, the vinegar to the second and the oil to the large hole. Then pour the water over everything, add the optional vegan chocolate chips and stir to combine.

Pour into the prepared pan and bake for 25 to 30 minutes, or until the top is springy and a toothpick inserted in the center comes out clean.

Cool the cake in the pan on a wire rack; then cut and serve. Keep at room temperature, wrapped airtight, for up to three days; refrigerate after that.

Warm Apple Crisp

Nut-free, soy-free
Splurge: Add ¼ cup (30 g) chopped pecans to the topping or serve with Coconut Whipped Cream (page 190)
Serves 6–8 · 60 minutes to prepare, plus time to cool

◗ • ◖

When apples are abundant, this is the perfect dessert. Warm, crumbly and sweet, it makes the whole house smell like fall. This is also a great recipe when you need a gluten-free option. Just swap out the flour with a gluten-free variety and make sure your oats are gluten-free as well.

4 apples, peeled, cored, seeded and cut into ¼-inch (6-mm) wedges

¼ cup (36 g) brown sugar

½ tsp cinnamon

½ tsp cornstarch

Pinch of salt

Coconut Whipped Cream (page 190), for serving, optional

CRUMBLE TOPPING

¾ cup (60 g) rolled oats

½ cup (63 g) flour

¼ cup (36 g) light brown sugar

½ tsp cinnamon

⅛ tsp nutmeg

¼ tsp salt

Chopped pecans, optional

½ cup (115 g) vegan butter, cut in small chunks and chilled

Preheat the oven to 375°F (191°C).

In a medium bowl, toss the apples, brown sugar, cinnamon, cornstarch and salt. Pour into a 9-inch (23-cm) pie pan.

Using the same bowl, combine the rolled oats, flour, light brown sugar, cinnamon, nutmeg, salt and optional chopped pecans for the topping. Add the cubed butter, working it into small chunks with either a fork or a pastry knife. The butter chunks should be no bigger than a pea.

Top the apples with the crumble topping, gently pressing the topping into the apples. You'll have a mound of apples and topping.

Bake for 45 to 50 minutes or until topping is golden brown. Remove from the oven and let cool for at least 30 minutes before serving.

TIP: We like to use a combination of sweet and tart apples.

Chocolate Coconut Cream Puffs

Nut-free, soy-free
Splurge: none
Makes approximately 20 cream puffs • 90 minutes to prepare

- • -

A chocolate cream puff. Does it get more decadent?! We like to make them bite size: the perfect portion of rich, creamy and oh-so-fluffy. It's hard to believe all that fanciness is the product of a very ordinary (accidentally vegan) canned biscuit. It can be our little secret.

1 cup (130 g) powdered sugar

4 tbsp (28 g) unsweetened cocoa powder

Pinch of salt

3 tbsp (45 ml) nondairy milk

1 tsp pure vanilla extract

1 cup (240 ml) canola oil

1 (7.5-oz [210-g]) can biscuits

Coconut Whipped Cream (page 190)

To make the chocolate glaze, whisk the powdered sugar, cocoa powder and salt in a medium bowl. Add the nondairy milk and vanilla extract and whisk until smooth. Set aside until you're ready to assemble.

Warm the canola oil in a small, heavy-bottomed saucepan over medium-low heat. If you have a thermometer, you'll want the oil around 365°F (185°C). Otherwise you can put the handle of a wooden spoon into the oil. When tiny little bubbles form around it, the oil is ready.

Cut the biscuits into tiny rounds. The lid of a spice jar works nicely. When the oil is hot enough (and please do be careful), drop a few of the biscuit rounds into the oil. Cook for about 45 seconds each side, depending on how hot your oil is.

Transfer the cooked puffs to a paper towel–lined plate to cool. Cut the first few open to make sure they're not still doughy on the inside. If they're doughy on the inside and sufficiently browned on the outside, your oil is too hot. Make adjustments and keep working through all of the dough rounds.

When all of the puffs are completely cooked, gently cut the puffs almost in half. With a small butter knife, add a dollop of the Coconut Whipped Cream so it's just peeking out when you close them up.

Ever so gently, dip the top of the puffs into the chocolate glaze. If the glaze is too thick for dipping, whisk in a little extra nondairy milk. You can also drizzle the tops if dipping is problematic. Chocolate cream puffs are best served immediately.

Rustic Pear Galette

Nut-free, soy-free
Splurge: Top with Coconut Whipped Cream (page 190)
Serves 8 · 60 minutes to prepare

•••

It's no secret that making fanciful pies with those little hand-cut leaves is not what I'm good at. But I still love pie, and the galette is the perfect solution: low stress, all of the essential pie elements, and beautiful in its own homespun way. Bonus points that it's adaptable to just about any fruit that's in season or that you might have on hand. —Katie

Flaky Pie Crust (page 189)

3 tbsp (36 g) sugar

½ tsp cinnamon

4–5 ripe pears, peeled, halved, cored and sliced thin

2 tbsp (16 g) powdered sugar, for serving, optional

Coconut Whipped Cream (page 190), for serving, optional

Preheat the oven to 375°F (191°C). Line a baking sheet with parchment paper.

On a clean surface, dusted with flour, roll out your dough in a circle about ¼-inch (6-mm) thick and 12 to 14 inches (30 to 36 cm) in diameter. It's rustic, so it doesn't need to be perfect. Now carefully fold your dough circle in half, and then in half again, so it's easy to pick up and transfer to the lined baking sheet without ripping. Refrigerate until ready to assemble your galette.

In a small bowl, combine the sugar and cinnamon. Toss with the pears in a large bowl until evenly coated.

Remove the dough from the refrigerator and unfold into a circle. Pour the pears out onto the middle of the dough. Just maintain a 1½- to 2-inch (38- to 51-mm) border. Fold and pleat the dough border onto the pears, pinching where the folds come together. The center will be open.

Bake for about 35 minutes, or until the crust is browned. Let cool for at least 20 minutes before serving. Dust lightly with powdered sugar and top with Coconut Whipped Cream, if using.

See image on page 170.

Flaky Pie Crust

Nut-free, soy-free
Splurge: none
Makes 2 dough rounds • 45 minutes to prepare

- • -

The key to a light and flaky crust is keeping tiny little chunks of your butter intact throughout your dough. Vegan butter is naturally softer than dairy butter, so a successful crust requires a little extra chilling to prevent the dough from becoming too homogenous.

1½ cups (344 g) vegan butter, such as Earth Balance butter

⅓ cup (78 ml) ice cold water and more if dough is too crumbly

2 cups (250 g) flour

¼ tsp salt

Cube the butter and freeze, about an hour. Also, chill your water in the freezer for about 20 minutes.

Add flour and salt to the large bowl of a food processor. Add the chilled butter, pulsing to combine until you have pea-sized pieces. Slowly add the cold water, until the dough just comes together. Turn your dough out onto a clean work surface.

Divide the dough in half. Quickly and gently shape into flat rounds. Wrap in plastic wrap and refrigerate at least 4 hours. Overnight is best.

Coconut Whipped Cream

Nut-free, soy-free, gluten-free
Splurge: none
Makes 2 cups (152 g) whipped cream • 15 minutes to prepare, plus 8 hours to chill coconut cream

● ● ◄

Before some brilliant vegan decided to whip coconut cream, the options were slim and a bit dull in the taste department. The delicate coconut flavor makes this vegan staple even better than the real thing: perfect for dipping fresh fruit or topping your favorite dessert.

1 (15-oz [425-g]) can coconut cream, chilled 8 hours

2 tbsp (16 g) powdered sugar

1 tsp vanilla

Chill your bowl and beater(s) in the freezer for 15 minutes before starting.

Open your chilled can of coconut cream. Pour off the water that has separated from the cream.

Add the cream, powdered sugar and vanilla to the bowl of a mixer fitted with the whisk attachment. Mix until fluffy, about 2 to 3 minutes.

Return the coconut whipped cream to the refrigerator until ready to use.

TIP: You can substitute maple syrup or agave for the powdered sugar. Make it chocolate whipped cream by adding 1 or 2 tablespoons (7 or 14 g) of cocoa powder.

Graham Cracker Pie Crust

Nut-free, soy-free
Splurge: none
Makes one 9-inch (23-cm) pie crust or 12 mini pie crusts • 10 minutes to prepare

● • ◄

Some desserts just don't work without a graham cracker crust. Though this recipe is specifically designed to go with our Mini Key Lime Pies (page 179), you'll find yourself coming back to it for other plant-based desserts that need a simple, delicious base. When shopping for graham crackers, be sure to check the ingredients, as many contain honey. Nabisco makes an "accidentally vegan" variety you can find in most major grocery stores.

1¼ cups (112 g) graham cracker crumbs

⅛ tsp sea salt

¼ cup (60 ml) coconut oil, melted

Preheat the oven to 350°F (177°C) and fit a muffin tin with paper liners.

Put the graham crackers and sea salt in a food processor and pulse several times until the mixture is very fine. Slowly stream in the coconut oil and process until well combined. Distribute the mixture into the muffin tin liners or pie tin; press down very firmly with your fingers (or the back of a spoon) until the crust is tight and compact.

Bake for 5 minutes, or until golden brown. Set aside to cool and use with our Mini Key Lime Pies (page 179).

MORE SMART SHOPPING

The reigning perception is that being vegan is expensive. Sure, it can be. But it definitely doesn't have to be. There are a few things we plant eaters tend to consume en masse that can easily be swapped out for more financially responsible alternates. Here are a few of our favorite swaps.

GRAINS, LEGUMES, SEEDS AND NUTS

INSTEAD OF THIS . . .	EAT THIS!	WHEN TO SWAP
Kasha ($7.20/lb)	Wheat berries ($4.80/lb), pearl barley ($4.96/lb)	In stuffing, side dishes, soups or stews, salads
Amaranth ($8.64/lb)	Couscous ($2.56/lb), millet ($5.12/lb)	In soups or stews, salads, stuffed peppers, side dishes
Quinoa ($8.64/lb)	Couscous ($2.56/lb), brown rice ($2.88/lb), millet ($5.12/lb), bulgur ($2.40/lb), buckwheat groats ($4.80/lb)	Salads, side dishes, soups or stews
Freekeh ($11.52/lb)	Wheat berries ($4.80/lb), bulgur ($2.40/lb), couscous ($2.56/lb), spelt berries ($2.56/lb), kamut berries ($5.92/lb)	In salads, casseroles, soups or stews, pilafs
Farro ($6.88/lb)	Wheat berries ($4.80/lb), bulgur ($2.40/lb), couscous ($2.56/lb), spelt berries ($2.56/lb), kamut berries ($5.92/lb)	In salads, soups or stews, side dishes
French green lentils ($4.32/lb)	Brown lentils ($2.08/lb), red lentils ($2.88/lb), split green peas ($2.08/lb)	In soups or stews, side dishes
Cannellini beans ($9.32/lb)	Great northern beans ($2.72/lb), navy beans ($2.91/lb)	In soups or stews, casseroles, dips, hummus
Chia seed ($7.49/lb)	Golden flax seed ($2.86/lb)	Egg replacement, salad dressings, smoothies
Hemp seed ($11.04/lb)	Chia seed ($7.49/lb)	Smoothies, shakes, hot cereals, salads, baked goods
Raw cashews ($7.49/lb)	Almonds ($6.33/lb)	Nut-based cheeses, salads, trail mix
Pine nuts ($31.20/lb)	Pumpkin seeds ($8.80/lb), sunflower seeds ($2.88/lb)	Pesto, salads, trail mix

*Resource: Amazon Prime Pantry

OILS AND VINEGARS

INSTEAD OF THIS . . .	EAT THIS!	WHEN TO SWAP
Avocado oil ($0.58/fl oz)	Extra-virgin olive oil ($0.48/fl oz)	Salad dressings, but not cooking
Extra-virgin olive oil ($0.48/fl oz)	Vegetable oil ($0.06/fl oz), canola oil ($0.10/fl oz)	Salad dressings
Grapeseed oil ($0.56/fl oz)	Vegetable oil ($0.06/fl oz), canola oil ($0.10/fl oz), corn oil ($0.06/fl oz), peanut oil ($0.16/fl oz)	High-heat cooking
Coconut oil ($0.43/fl oz)	Vegetable oil ($0.06/fl oz), canola oil ($0.10/fl oz)	Cookies, brownies, cakes, muffins

Sunflower oil ($0.43/fl oz)	Vegetable oil ($0.06/fl oz), canola oil ($0.10/fl oz), corn oil ($0.06/fl oz)	High-heat cooking, cookies, brownies, cakes, muffins
Toasted sesame oil ($0.64/fl oz)	Peanut oil ($0.16/fl oz)	Asian cooking
Champagne vinegar ($0.44/fl oz)	White wine vinegar ($0.21/fl oz)	Salad dressings
Balsamic vinegar ($0.21/fl oz)	Red wine vinegar ($0.16/fl oz), apple cider vinegar ($0.17/fl oz)	Salad dressings, marinades, chutneys
Apple cider vinegar ($0.17/fl oz)	White vinegar ($0.06/fl oz)	Pickling, mustards, salad dressings

*Resource: Amazon Prime Pantry

FRUITS AND VEGETABLES

INSTEAD OF THIS . . .	EAT THIS!	WHEN TO SWAP
Asparagus ($0.20/oz)	Green beans ($0.13/oz)	Side dishes
Baby bella mushrooms ($0.38/oz)	White button mushrooms ($0.21/oz)	Stir-fries, quesadillas, pizza toppings
Blueberries ($0.29/oz)	Cherries ($0.22/oz), pomegranate ($0.13/oz)	Fruit salads, cereal toppings
Butternut squash ($0.07/oz)	Sweet potato ($0.05/oz)	Soups or stews, chili, pilafs, side dishes
Okra ($0.20/oz)	Brussels sprouts ($0.17/oz)	Side dishes, roasted veggies
Red bell peppers ($0.14/oz)	Green bell peppers ($0.08/oz)	Stuffed peppers, soups or stews, stir-fries
Spinach ($0.23/oz)	Kale ($0.17/oz)	Salads, soups or stews, bowls, side dishes

*Resource: USDA Economic Research Service Fruit and Vegetable Prices, 2013

MISCELLANEOUS

INSTEAD OF THIS . . .	EAT THIS!	WHEN TO SWAP
Cashew cream ($4.65/14 oz)*	Coconut cream ($2.29/14 oz)	Soups, sauces, dips
Fake ground meat crumbles ($5.59/11 oz)	Texturized vegetable protein (TVP) ($2.99/48 oz prepared or 16 oz dried)	Soups or stews, chili, tacos
Cashew butter ($14.78/16 oz) or almond butter ($12.34/16 oz)	Sunflower seed butter ($10.25/16 oz)	Sandwiches, toast
Maple syrup ($9.49/12 oz)	Maple/agave-blend syrup ($5.50/11.75 oz)	Baked goods, sauces, pancakes

*You need about 2 cups (222 g) of raw cashews to make 14 ounces (397 g) cashew cream.

It's important to note that grocery prices can vary quite a bit depending on where you live and the stores at which you shop. For example, you might find that farro is more affordable than wheat berries at your local Trader Joe's. Or perhaps your neighborhood produce market is having a crazy sale on asparagus, but the price of green beans has skyrocketed. Of course, if you choose to buy everything organic at Whole Foods, your grocery prices will definitely be higher than ours. The point of the tables (pages 192 to 193) is to provide a general reference point and to show you that saving money can be as easy as thinking outside the (recipe) box.

Another thing we want to mention is that just because you're on a budget, it doesn't mean you have to stick to foods in the "Eat this!" column. In fact, many of the recipes in this book have the option to use pricier ingredients—and you can, too! Keeping it affordable is all about creating a balance with cheaper foods. For example, our Thai Peanut Sauce (page 156) contains toasted sesame oil, which can cost as much as ten dollars a bottle. Yikes, right? We bring the cost per serving down by pairing it with soy sauce, peanut butter, rice vinegar and lime juice, which are all super affordable. Not to mention, our Thai Peanut Sauce only uses 1 teaspoon of sesame oil, which comes out to just $0.09 for the recipe. At this rate, a 16 fluid ounce (473 ml) bottle of sesame oil would last you at least a year!

START A FRIDGE TRIAGE BOX

Be honest. How many times have you opened your crisper drawer and pulled out an unopened bag of spinach that had turned a lovely shade of brown? If you're like most folks, it happens more often than you'd like to admit. In fact, the average U.S. consumer wastes more than 20 pounds (9 kg) of food each month. When you consider that fruits and vegetables make up a majority of a vegan diet, that's a lot of fresh, beautiful produce you're tossing into the trash.

Not only is food waste terrible for the environment, but throwing away five pounds (2.2 kg) of produce each week is an inefficient use of your grocery budget. How inefficient? Given the fact that American households throw away an average of $640 worth of food each year, you might as well be tossing $53 per month in your compost bin. That's a pretty significant chunk of change! So, what can you do to stop being wasteful and keep some of that hard-earned cash in your pocket? We're happy to report that there's a super easy way to stop wasting so much food and drastically reduce the amount of money you spend at the supermarket. Introducing: the fridge triage box.

WHAT IS A FRIDGE TRIAGE BOX?
It's an effective visual cue that reminds you of the food in your refrigerator that's nearing its expiration date. You know, the celery, apples and radishes that were tucked beneath that takeout container. It will totally change the way you and your family view and consume the food in your fridge.

WHY DO I NEED ONE?
One of the main reasons why food items rot in your refrigerator is because you forget you have them. Your carrots and kale are hidden away in a special drawer that's supposed to keep them fresh (go figure). But by moving all of the food that needs to be eaten pronto into a centralized, eye-level location, you're more likely to eat it before it goes bad.

COOL! HOW DO I GET STARTED?
All you need to get started with your fridge triage box is a plastic bin (they're easier to clean than an actual cardboard box) and a sign that says "Eat Me First!" or something like that. Then, go through your entire refrigerator and fill the bin with fruits, vegetables and herbs that are nearing their expiration dates. You can add the produce to our Tofu Scrambled Eggs (page 124), simmer it in our Minestrone (page 100) or slice it up and add it to our Roasted Potato and Zucchini Pizza (page 25). You'd be surprised at how well this actually works!

BUILDING A BUDGET PANTRY

Having a solid pantry full of budget-friendly items is a great way to save money on food. For one, it helps avoid unnecessary trips to the grocery store, which prevents you from making impulse purchases on stuff you don't really need (like that six-dollar kombucha). And, if you have plenty of food on hand to whip something up at home, you'll be less tempted to pick up that takeout menu. We love ordering vegan pizza as much as the next person, but those delivery fees and tips add up.

Building a budget pantry doesn't have to be overwhelming, and you don't have to do it all at once. When staples with a long shelf life are on sale, stock up! Keeping your pantry organized will be key to saving money, too. If you can clearly see everything you have, you won't buy more than you need. Store your bulk items in labeled glass or BPA-free plastic containers, and arrange your canned goods by expiration date so you're sure to eat the oldest stuff first.

The items below are all good things to have on hand for making breakfast, lunch or dinner on a whim. You'll also see many of them throughout the recipes in this book, so feel free to use this page as a shopping list.

CANNED GOODS

- Black beans
- Kidney beans
- Garbanzo beans
- White beans
- Pinto beans
- Coconut milk
- Pumpkin purée

- Diced tomatoes
- Crushed tomatoes
- Tomato sauce
- Tomato paste
- Extra-virgin olive oil
- Canola oil or vegetable oil

- Toasted sesame oil
- Balsamic vinegar
- Apple cider vinegar
- Rice vinegar
- Red wine vinegar

DRY GOODS

- Brown rice
- Couscous
- Spaghetti
- Penne
- Rice noodles

- Dried pinto beans
- Dried black beans
- Dried kidney beans
- Dried white beans
- Dried garbanzo beans

- Brown lentils
- Red lentils
- Split green peas
- Chia seeds
- Sunflower seeds

BAKING

- All-purpose flour
- Whole wheat flour
- Cocoa powder
- Rolled oats
- Coconut sugar*

- Baking powder
- Baking soda
- Cornstarch
- Tapioca flour
- Maple syrup

- Agave nectar
- Vanilla extract
- Instant yeast

SPICES

- Sea salt
- Black pepper
- Basil
- Oregano
- Rosemary
- Thyme

- Cayenne pepper
- Cumin
- Cinnamon
- Turmeric
- Curry powder
- Nutmeg

- Paprika
- Chili powder
- Garlic powder
- Red pepper flakes

MISCELLANEOUS

- Nutritional yeast
- Minced garlic
- Hot sauce
- Bouillon cubes, such as Better Than Bouillon

- Applesauce
- Soy sauce
- Tamari
- Dijon mustard
- Miso paste

- Liquid smoke
- Nondairy milk
- Peanut butter
- Pasta sauce

This list might look long and intimidating, but don't stress. Purchase a few items per week until your pantry is full and you won't even notice the dent in your grocery bill. And please, shop within your means. Just because an item is on this list doesn't mean you absolutely have to buy it.

We like coconut sugar because it contains antioxidants and packs impressive nutrients, like zinc and iron. However, it can be swapped for ordinary cane sugar in most recipes.

HOW TO KEEP IT ORGANIC (OR DO YOUR BEST)

We all know that eating organic is better for us and better for the environment. But eating organic on a budget can be tricky. When looking for cost-effective ways to bring home organics, try buying fruits and vegetables from the freezer section. Frozen produce is picked and frozen at the peak of ripeness and often has higher levels of vitamins and cancer-fighting antioxidants than its fresh or canned counterparts. For example, 1 cup (180 g) of frozen spinach has four times the amount of nutrients (fiber, folate, iron and calcium) than a cup of fresh spinach. That being said, we get that there are some frozen vegetables that just turn to mush (broccoli, asparagus and mushrooms, for example). Avoid those and focus on the choices that defrost perfectly: corn, peas, spinach, pearl onions, berries and other fruits (for compotes and smoothies).

Another option for keeping on budget is to join a local CSA. Split a box with a neighbor to make it more cost-effective and avoid any wasted produce at the end of the week. From our experience, it's usually a ridiculous amount of local, organic produce for the price. Using it all up is the key to value there. So be prepared to get creative and explore some new and unique produce from your region.

If you aren't afraid of a little dirt under your fingernails, gardening is a great opportunity for staying on budget and eating organic all summer long. To start, you don't need much more than dirt and seeds. Patio gardeners will need to make a modest investment in some planters or pots, but don't be dissuaded—you can find very inexpensive options.

If this is your first foray into growing food, start small. Plan your garden and find what works for your schedule and your climate before you get in too deep (*The Old Farmer's Almanac* is a great resource). Planting a lot means finding the time to take care of all that radical vegetation; from preparing to planting, watering and harvesting. But it's all worth it, as a few snips of just about any fresh herb will take your budget cooking to the next level.

Don't have a yard? Community gardens are a great choice. Meet some neighbors, drink some beer and have your own built-in CSA.

For most of us, buying organic everything just isn't an option. When you are buying non-organic produce, you'll want to give it a good soak to remove as much pesticide residue as possible. Use 1 tablespoon (15 ml) of apple cider vinegar for every cup (240 ml) of water and let sit at least 5 minutes before rinsing well. If you need to prioritize, use the list below. These are the most important things to buy organic.

- Apples
- Peaches
- Nectarines
- Strawberries
- Grapes
- Celery

- Spinach
- Sweet bell peppers
- Cucumbers
- Cherry tomatoes
- Snap peas (imported)
- Potatoes

- Hot peppers
- Kale
- Collard greens

Acknowledgments

— • —

First and foremost, we would like to express our gratitude to Page Street Publishing for giving us the opportunity to share our passion for affordable, plant-based cooking. Especially our editor, Elizabeth Seise, for providing outstanding support to two first-time authors. We'd also like to thank our photographer, Allie Lehman, for adopting our vision for this book and working tirelessly to accommodate our requests for "More sauce, please!" and "Can you make it look more gooey?" across three time zones.

We are so appreciative of our fabulous designer, Mette Hornung Rankin of the Bureau of Betterment, for her assistance in developing the Well Vegan brand and designing the cover of this book. Special thanks to the instructors at Matthew Kenney Culinary. Finally, we'd like to thank our families and closest friends who supported us, endured endless taste tests and even washed the dishes for us throughout the course of writing this cookbook. We couldn't have published these recipes without you.

About the Authors

KATIE KOTEEN

Katie Koteen is the founder, photographer and meal planner behind Well Vegan, a vegan meal-planning service that makes it easy and affordable to follow a plant-based diet.

Though she currently resides in the most vegan-friendly city in America, Katie's food experience began on the dusty prairies of the Midwest. With almost four decades of regionally diverse eating experience, she enjoys the challenge of feeding a vegan family on a budget and is sleep deprived enough to consider meal planning a hobby. You'll often find her in the kitchen testing new recipes, her trusty hound at her side eager to devour the fails.

Katie lives in Portland, Oregon with her husband and their two kids.

KATE KASBEE

Kate Kasbee is the recipe developer and content creator behind Well Vegan and the author of *Well Vegan: A Starter Guide*.

A true midwesterner, Kate considers pizza to be its own food group and feels most at home in the kitchen, cooking for whoever is willing to try her latest recipe. Though she's always been obsessed with food, Kate's passion for vegan cuisine really took hold while attending Matthew Kenney Culinary in Thailand, where she became a certified plant-based chef. A wanderer at heart, Kate's recipes are inspired by her travels and the flavors of her favorite parts of the world.

Kate lives in Chicago, Illinois, with her small dog and a massive collection of spices.

Index